GREETINGS FROM UTOPIA PARK

Greetings from Utopia Park

SURVIVING A TRANSCENDENT CHILDHOOD

Claire Hoffman

HARPER

An Imprint of HarperCollins*Publishers*

FIRST EDITION

All photographs, unless otherwise indicated, are courtesy of the author.

Designed by Adam B. Bohannon

Library of Congress Cataloging-in-Publication Data has been applied for.

ISBN: 978-0-06-233884-6

16 17 18 19 20   OV/RRD   10 9 8 7 6 5 4 3 2 1

To my mom, who believed in Utopia,
and to my daughters,
who forced me to see
it could be true.

Author's Note

This is not an official history of the Transcendental Meditation Movement nor of the Maharishi. It's my memory of my experience. I've bolstered those memories with archival research and interviews. Names have been changed upon request.

Contents

Part Three: Searching

Preface

In the end, I went back to Iowa because I thought somehow the past held the answer to my future. I was at the age when fears were taking hold—fear of becoming my mother, fear of not being as good as my mother, fear of becoming an adult and letting go of everything that had made my childhood vivid and hopeful, mystical and turmeric scented. In leaving behind a world where spending hours a day meditating was the norm, I had ended up with an adult life that felt empty of the quiet sacredness I had taken for granted as a kid. Around me, it felt like everyone was starting to meditate and practice yoga—things that when I was growing up had marked me as an outsider in our divided Midwestern town.

That summer, I was thirty-four years old and a new mom and a new wife. I was a writer for *Rolling Stone* and had an assistant professor position at UC Riverside, just south of Los Angeles, where I'd lived for six years. I had worked hard to get to where I was but everything I'd strived for increasingly felt like a burden. I was perpetually exhausted and anxious and I couldn't shake a looming sense of dissatisfaction. I had a sense that I'd let something precious slip through my fingers. Had I made a mistake? Somewhere along the line, in trying to be a normal person, had I let go of who I was?

This felt particularly troubling for me since I'd grown up practicing Transcendental Meditation and had for a long time believed that I was immune to problems like stress and depression. Though

I meditated sporadically, I figured a lifetime of practice would have created some sort of immunity. By my own very rough calculations, I'd spent more than 2,200 hours of my life meditating.

It was around this time that something odd began to happen to me. Growing up, the people I knew who had sought out Transcendental Meditation had been former hippies—my mom and her friends who were interested in consciousness and creating world peace. That impulse felt to me like something from another generation—a faded Age of Aquarius dream. I'd lived away from Iowa for seventeen years, and no one had asked me about learning to meditate. But now, people like Katy Perry and Russell Simmons and Rupert Murdoch were tweeting about how great TM was, how transformed their lives had become. And people kept asking me about it. Did I like it, did it work, where could they learn it, would it make them happier?

This confluence of events—my own malaise, my struggle with how to be an adult and a good parent, and the resurgence of TM in the zeitgeist put the idea in my head that I needed to go home. And I needed to learn how to fly.

Meditation has always been complicated for me. Transcendental Meditation was the cornerstone of our community, but the promise was that from there you would graduate into an entire world where everything had meaning and significance. Transcendental Meditation was a product sold by our guru, Maharishi Mahesh Yogi, but he had ambitions to take people beyond the twenty minutes a day to another level of meditation, an extended practice that promised greater power and new levels of awareness and joy. By practicing his extended form of meditation, my community thought they were ushering in Heaven on Earth.

I am generally described as a down-to-earth and practical person, but what I decided to do that summer did not seem so logical. In order to reorient myself, I went home to the small rural Midwestern community I'd grown up in and started lessons for the secretive meditation technique that promised the ability to levitate—and create world peace.

And so it was that I found myself inside a dingy basement in my hometown of Fairfield, Iowa, hoping that I would somehow shed my heavily accrued cynicism and fly. Outside the small overhead windows, I could see the rain pouring down, the sky flashing with lightning. But in here, the air was dim, cool, and heavy with the scent of burning sandalwood. The entire room, from wall to wall, was covered in a carpet of thick foam. Each piece was wrapped in a saggy white cotton sheet. It felt like a giant adult jumpy house. Women of various ages, in various stages of repose, sat along the perimeter of the space, surrounded by a mishmash of pillows.

I bounce-walked my way across the room and took my seat among them, giving smiles to those who gave them to me. I turned my eyes to the woman in the corner who wore a brightly colored green sari.

"All right, my little chickadees," she said in a voice that made me think of Glinda the Good Witch. "Today we fly!" On the wall above her was a large hand-painted banner that read "Yogic Flying Competition," the letters majestic and golden.

She rang her bell and silence followed. We closed our eyes. I heard the rumble of thunder. There was a slumber-party sort of anything could happen breathlessness in the air. Anything could happen. And soon it did. Across the room, a girl began a low sort of ecstatic moaning. I opened one eye. Around me everyone was perfectly still, eyes shut, faces fixed in concentrated contemplation. Except for the woman moaning. Her body was starting to shudder and sway, almost convulsively.

This lady is totally faking it, I thought. But then her body began to rock up and down in the air. I shut my eyes. I didn't want to watch anymore. I didn't want to judge her. I could hear her butt smacking against the foam as she rocked up and down. I couldn't bear to watch. I wanted to do it myself. I wanted to fly.

"Believe," I whispered in my head. "You have to believe."

PART ONE

Believing

CHAPTER ONE

Initiation

"I want to be initiated now," I announced, staring into the eyes of the teacher.

We were gathered at an office of the Transcendental Meditation Center in Manhattan for the ceremony in which my older brother, Stacey, was meant to get his mantra, a secret phrase all his own to chant quietly to himself every day. This mantra would have been Stacey's first step in his path to Enlightenment. But Stacey, five years old, seemed intimidated and overwhelmed by the ceremony and, when the time came for him to be alone with the teacher, he was resolute: he wouldn't do it.

I knew that this teacher could bestow special powers.

"I want to learn my mantra today," I told him. I wanted that power.

Then I turned to my mother.

"I'm not leaving."

Normally, I was a compliant child, eager to please and slow to speak up—but I was certain enough about this, even at three, to take a stand.

My parents, Liz and Fred, had both been followers of the Indian guru Maharishi Mahesh Yogi and practitioners of Transcendental Meditation throughout their twenties, but these days only my mother continued the practice. My father I saw less often—and when I did, the fermented smell of booze wafted off him as he stumbled through our apartment late at night.

I knew that meditation connected you to another realm. Every evening, I watched my mom close the old warped glass living room doors and sit on our couch, covered in a paisley shawl, her legs folded Indian style, her eyes closed. She never moved, never made a sound. To me, she looked like a king from one of my books, seated on her throne. Receiving my mantra would be my entrée into the secret world she had been slipping into—away from me—throughout my life. This was my chance to follow her to wherever she went, to become like her, to be silent and majestic, to become a king.

At the TM offices, the instructor told us we needed a fresh set of fruit and flowers as offerings for my initiation. Stacey's offering had apparently already been drained of its value. My mother led my brother and me downstairs to a bodega, where we bought a few wilted carnations, a bruised apple, and some oranges. When we returned, I followed the teacher to a dingy back office furnished with two tired-looking easy chairs draped with golden scarves. A red Oriental rug lay over the thin gray carpet; incense was burning.

The man helped me climb into a chair, my feet dangling off the floor, and he sat beside me, the two of us facing a large photograph of Maharishi's teacher, Guru Dev, a wizened Indian man. At home we had the same picture, as well as lots of pictures of Maharishi with his crinkly smile. I would stare at his face and marvel at how his flowing beard and long hair merged into a waterfall-like mane encircling his head. Maharishi seemed always to be holding roses with light radiating from his head. I thought of him as the most important and powerful member of our family—after all, his picture hung alongside my parents' wedding photo. I also considered him part of a powerful trilogy: Yoda. Santa. Maharishi. All of them old, all-knowing, magical.

The teacher carefully placed my bodega gifts in front of a small altar near Maharishi's image, and then he began to speak to me in a lilting voice, as if he was reading from a script.

"I will tell you one Word of Wisdom—this will be your own private Word of Wisdom. You would like to have it?" he asked.

I nodded.

"And you want to become great and do great things? Yes?"

I nodded again.

"Yes, you will become a great lady with your Word of Wisdom and you will repeat it a few times each day; but do you know one thing, everyone keeps their Word of Wisdom very secret—you will keep it to yourself, you will not tell it to your friends or to anyone, yes?"

I nodded again. I knew that a mantra was the most secret of things and that everyone's was different, like snowflakes. This was why I wanted it!

He continued: "You know, everyone keeps the key to his treasury in his own pocket and doesn't give it to anyone else. So this Word of Wisdom is the key to all wisdom in life. I know you are very intelligent—you won't tell it to anyone. Yes?" I nodded hard. Yes, I could keep secrets.

"All right. Now we will make offerings to Guru Dev who gave this Word of Wisdom to Maharishi and Maharishi has given it to me and I will give it to you." He nudged me closer to the altar. Propped up in the middle of the tableau was a painting with a lush river wending its way down its center. On either side of the river were Indian men in robes, sitting in the lotus position, with gold beams emanating from their heads. There was a little figure of Maharishi who stood with his hands in prayer in front of Guru Dev, who sat on a golden throne at the base of the river. I knew Guru Dev was Maharishi's teacher and that he had lived in a cave in the woods. And that he was super Enlightened. And dead.

"This is the Holy Tradition," he said. "So according to the custom of the Holy Tradition, I will make offerings to Guru Dev and then we will tell you the word, yes?

"Come with me—stand here—take this flower in your hand and witness the ceremony. I am sure you will like it."

Then he started chanting words I didn't understand in a language I'd never heard. When he turned to face me, his eyelids fluttered as if he was about to fall asleep. He bowed to the picture of Guru Dev, motioning for me to follow suit.

He said that I was to say my Word of Wisdom mantra silently to myself every day for five minutes in the morning and five minutes at night and allow whatever happened inside my head to happen. Mother Nature would ensure that it was just as it should be! I didn't need to close my eyes or sit still while I did this—I could walk or draw, but I couldn't talk. He whispered a sound to me, and I said it back. It would be more than a decade before I would say it out loud again. Now, he told me, say it inside your head. I did. It felt like it was ringing out in the darkness. I tried to feel inside my body for some kind of change.

"This is how you will be saying it to yourself, moving the tongue inside, while getting ready for school and for a few minutes before you do your lessons or play; with your Word of Wisdom you will become very creative. And you know you will keep it secret, to yourself?" I nodded, feeling entirely grown up. I didn't have homework or lessons, but now I had a mantra. I rolled it over in my mind like a stone. He took the offerings I'd brought and handed them to me. "Now you will take this fruit and keep this handkerchief and flower and go and walk about saying your word quietly and I will see you in ten minutes to check your pronunciation before you go home."

I loved it. I felt it change what was happening inside my head—my thoughts slowed down. I sensed that I had tapped into something powerful and important. I stayed in that room, with the incense burning, and quietly repeated the sound inside my mind. When the time was up, my teacher returned and whispered, "Jai Guru Dev," in a deep, serious voice. He told me this meant praises to Guru Dev, who had handed down my secret sound just so I could have it. My body surged with the specialness of it as I ran out of the room to give my mom a hug. Stacey sat sullenly next to her, trying to ignore my spiritual triumph.

When we walked out onto Lexington Avenue, horns were blaring and people were talking, and my mom and brother were arguing about what we would do next as the dirty snow sprayed off the wheels of speeding taxis. But I felt important, lifted above the dull, anxious drone.

My mom told me her story of meeting Maharishi the way most people tell their kids about falling in love. It went something like this: On a crisp fall day in 1970, my mother stood near the back entrance of the University of Colorado auditorium, shyly clasping a pink carnation in her hands. She was a petite nineteen-year-old, with long shiny brown hair, glittering blue eyes, and an upturned nose that made her look forever baby faced. A cute boy from her art history class had invited her there, handing her an extra flower and telling her that a group of them were going to wait to greet the Maharishi and catch a glimpse of a real live guru.

My mom didn't even really know what that meant: *guru*. She had come to Boulder two years earlier seeking a new life. All she wanted out of college was to escape the tumult of her family back in Princeton, New Jersey. Her parents were the children of immigrants—German and Irish—who had seen the gleaming 1950s version of the American dream as a way to distance themselves from the working-class New York City ghettos where they'd grown up.

My grandfather Harry was a lanky, absentminded veteran who worked as an engineer for RCA and Princeton University. My grandmother Denny was an intense, wickedly funny, dark-haired nurse who worked part-time in emergency rooms. There'd always been jokes that she had a true Irish temper, but Denny took her anger over the edge. Her idea of parenting included lining the dining room table with knives taped to the rim, blade side up, in order to teach her two daughters not to rudely rest their elbows while eating. She would throw food at them if they didn't eat and would hit my mom for any host of unknown infractions. Mom lived in fear of her mother and her moods.

When my grandmother found out Harry was having an affair with my mom's guitar teacher, the couple took on divorce the old-fashioned way, making *Who's Afraid of Virginia Woolf?* look sentimental.

My grandmother's rage overtook their home. She threw my mother around and tried to strangle her for listening to the radio. Eventually Denny slit her wrists in front of her husband and, as he hustled her off to the hospital, my mom cleaned up her parents' blood-covered bedroom, working quickly so her kid sister—who spent her days in front of the TV—wouldn't see the mess.

My mom tuned out the hysteria by huddling in her room and listening to her Beatles albums, swept away by the lyrics of love and longing. She devoured everything she could read about the Fab Four, and she grew her hair long and shaggy. One day she read a *Saturday Evening Post* article about a consciousness-raising trip the Beatles took to Rishikesh with the Maharishi. What was consciousness, and how could she get it? she wondered. No one talked about such things in her Roman Catholic home where sin and guilt loomed like an ever-present storm.

My mom was a good student, skilled at math and art, and when she examined her college options, it was the University of Colorado that stood out. She loved to ski and had been working diligently after school to save up money to buy her own skis. But really, she chose the school because it was sixteen hundred miles away from all that darkness and drama in New Jersey.

In Boulder, she'd quickly discarded her skirts and penny loafers for Wranglers and ski sweaters. She was a new person in search of a new world. She wasn't alone—all around her, people were experimenting with altering their reality. Everyone on campus seemed to be talking about consciousness, about how the world was so much bigger than it seemed, that life could be so much more expansive than their parents had ever imagined. At the Boulder house parties she went to, in rooms filled with pot smoke and booze, Mom was often the sober one. Drinking made her uncomfortable. It was her mom's thing—it looked out of control and dangerous to her. She knew the Beatles had turned to something called Transcendental Meditation to alter their reality without drugs. So when a friend from class invited her to an introductory lecture on TM, she jumped at the chance.

In the crowded auditorium, a well-spoken man in a suit explained the experience of meditation as well as Maharishi's transcendental theory of the universe. In simple terms, he told the standing room only audience that all of existence was consciousness. From consciousness sprang all of life. Meditation was a tool that would take you to that most fundamental layer of consciousness, what the instructor called "Pure Consciousness." This was the source of all creation. The man explained matter-of-factly that when you meditate, the mind acts like a pebble, floating down to the bottom of the ocean. The TM mantra took you down to this place of Pure Consciousness, and the thinking mind brought you back up. The mantra took you to a place where there was no thought, just unity. Diving down to that state of consciousness, he said, would make you happier, more relaxed, more creative, more intelligent, and a host of other things.

It made so much sense to my mother—that all of consciousness and being sprang from an underlying layer of creation that served as the source for the universe. And the idea that life should be simple and joyous, without suffering, and that nature itself was inherently blissful—it was so organic and appealing, a comforting departure from the judgmental Catholicism that she'd been raised with.

When a TM teacher arrived in Boulder months later, Mom borrowed her roommate's fringed leather jacket and walked across town with the $35 initiation fee, money she'd saved while working at the local record shop. There, she received her mantra. The moment she repeated it inside herself, she felt different. "This is me!" she thought. Saying her mantra took her to a place that was so familiar, so intimate, so different from the chaos of the outside world. Transcending connected her, she felt, to her true self. She walked home on that sunny afternoon and felt so alive—and it felt like people noticed. Her transcendent afterglow was palpable.

Until the day that the cute boy from art history invited her to come see the guru, she'd never thought much about the man who was purported to be the master of the technique that made her feel so radiant, who had even taught the Beatles, and who had come to the United States from India with the plan to change the world. Others who practiced TM told her that Maharishi was the living embodiment of the highest state of consciousness: he was Enlightened. Still, she felt a little silly waiting like a groupie outside a rock concert, hoping to give the guru a flower.

A white car pulled up, a devotee opened the back door, and the Maharishi stepped onto the pavement.

"He's so small!" my mother thought.

Clothed in a single sheet of white silk, the holy man carried his usual bouquet of flowers, his face wide open to those around him. He shuffled past the line of people, accepting their trembling offerings and murmuring greetings. When he stopped in front of my mother, he paused and looked into her eyes. She was overwhelmed. It was electrifying. With a childhood marked by abuse, she had never imagined that another human being could feel both so powerful and so pure. She also felt something else: intense recognition. As strange as it seemed, she felt that he knew her truly. She handed him the flower, which he took with a sweet, soft smile. And then as he walked away, she began to cry.

I never knew Maharishi. Despite the fact that he lived at the center of our lives, he was always presented to me as beyond human, with scant biographical details offered to give him shape beyond that of a luminous outline. As a kid, I knew him as the man in the pictures, the man who had meditated for two years in a cave and then come to the West to teach all of us an ancient practice with the goal of transforming Earth to Heaven. We were blessed to follow his example. I knew that he had paused to look into my mom's sparkling blue eyes and forever shifted our destiny.

But later, as a journalist and as a graduate student in divinity school, I started to learn more about this figure who had for so long only been abstractly magnificent to me. I would learn about his parents and his education and his ambition, which had propelled him from a middle-class kid in India to a global guru with holdings of untold billions.

I would learn that thirty years before that day he met my mother, he was a young man in his twenties who himself gazed into the eyes of a guru and felt the electric recognition of destiny.

In 1940, Mahesh Varma was sitting on a porch with a group of friends outside a mountaintop home in northern India. The college student was hoping to glimpse the revered saint, Brahmananda Saraswati. Although he was dedicated to studying physics, Mahesh always had a sense of longing for a more fundamental truth. He longed to deepen the meaning of his provincial, ordinary life.

Mahesh had heard that the holy man he had come to see had attained true Enlightenment after decades of meditating in a small cave behind a waterfall, subsisting on seeds and salt. So he had come to the outskirts of Jabalpur where the saint was visiting an ashram.

It was monsoon season. The group of young men had come at daybreak but the sun had risen and now set and they were still waiting. When at last a car rattled past the monastery, the headlights illuminated for a moment the face of the celebrated yogi—he'd been sitting nearby them, unnoticed, meditating silently.

It was at this mythological-like moment that Mahesh, the round-faced son of a local administrator who was fascinated by science, said that he first knew he wanted to join India's tradition of holy men. This was a disruptive decision because, like much else in India, spiritual power was confined to certain castes. Mahesh was of an administrative caste, not Brahmin. He could pursue spirituality, but his caste would not allow him to claim the title of guru.

But the moment he met Brahmananda Saraswati, the man he would come to call Guru Dev, and begged to become his disciple, he renounced all worldly things, including his family history and his name. Guru Dev was a traditional master, devoted to the tenants of Advaitin philosophy. Preserved in Vedic scripture, it is one of the world's oldest collections of sacred texts, dating back to around 1100 BC. Advaitin philosophy fundamentally teaches nonduality or the oneness of everything, and that the ability to self-realize or transcend into oneness is possible within a human life.

I would learn as an adult that these scriptures are seen as the precursor and textual basis for Hinduism. The Vedas as a whole are a rich, bizarre, mystical, chaotic, and enchanting group of writings. The oldest book, the Rig Veda, is a beautiful collection of hymns composed by rishis, said to be ancient seers, connected to the eternal hum of the universe. Many believe the Vedas contain ancient wisdom that could make men into living gods.

At Guru Dev's insistence, Mahesh completed his education in physics and mathematics, then entered the ashram where, for the next decade, he worked around the clock for the guru as a secretary. Old videos and photographs show Mahesh intently working for his master—tending to his flowers, overseeing his correspondence, arranging audiences, and ringing bells for him when he entered a building.

On May 20, 1953, Guru Dev died. The story passed down over the decades by Mahesh's followers is that when Guru Dev's body was lowered into the holy river of the Ganges, Mahesh, heartbroken, dove in after him.

The following years of Mahesh's life are shrouded in mystery. Movement legend holds that he retired to a cave in the jungles of Uttarkashi, known as the "Valley of the Saints," eating twigs and berries and meditating for two years, after which "the impulse of Nature itself," as he would later put it, inspired him to go south, to the densely populated, booming cities of India. This decision has been celebrated, in the literature of his Movement, as a moment that changed the fate of the earth.

In the city of Trivandrum—at the invitation of a prominent local lawyer—he began to teach the meditation practice that Guru Dev had taught him. He started with small groups, but quickly his audiences grew to thousands. His message was fresh: Meditation, he told those who came to listen, was not only for monks and yogis but for the workingman. Mahesh had "revived" and "condensed" the Vedic knowledge of his renunciant masters and stripped it down to a simple mental technique that could be easily utilized by anyone in any culture. The average citizen, or "householders," as Mahesh fondly called them, could transcend the world around them and "go beyond" thoughts in order to experience a state of blissful nonattachment. No worldly renunciation was required.

The technique was a simple, mantra-based meditation. You sat down, and closed your eyes. After about thirty seconds, you repeated a mantra, a short sound, to yourself, gently, at no particular pace or frequency. You let the mantra come to you. If your mind wandered, then you just "gently returned" to the mantra. And that was it. You meditated for ten to twenty minutes in the morning and again in the evening. That was Transcendental Meditation, a term that he soon trademarked.

As his audiences grew, Mahesh became known as Maharishi. And then, in December 1957, four years after the death of Guru Dev, Maharishi Mahesh Yogi announced to a crowded audience in southern India that he would "bring the Wisdom of the Vedic tradition to the whole world." He said he was starting a movement, the Spiritual Regeneration Movement. "Why can't we spiritually regenerate the world through this technique?" he asked, answered by thunderous applause. With that, he packed his few belongings in a deerskin rug, raised just enough money from local devotees for a plane ticket, and flew out of India, penniless.

When Maharishi Mahesh Yogi arrived in the Honolulu airport on the last day of 1958, wearing only his robe and exhibiting the bubbly laugh that would eventually lead to the nickname "the Giggling Guru," he declared his intention to make meditation a global practice. The *Honolulu Star-Bulletin* wrote that day, "He has no money; he asks for nothing. His worldly possessions can be carried in one hand. Maharishi Mahesh Yogi is on a world odyssey. He carries a message that he says will rid the world of unhappiness and discontent. . . ."

Maharishi arrived in the U.S. just as a whole generation was searching for something bigger and more meaningful than the middle-class American dream. Those young people were open to Maharishi's image of gentle purity and simple Eastern living as a new path different from their parents'. Maharishi promised his followers they could attain a higher state of consciousness, just like him.

*   *   *

In the decades to come, Maharishi traveled the world, always funded by wealthy donors, who came to him like moths to a flame. His followers now called him His Holiness Maharishi Mahesh Yogi. He established headquarters in Santa Barbara, California. His disciples printed up thousands of flyers advertising classes to learn "the simple, life-changing technique," then plastered them on kiosks at colleges across America. Students came in droves, paying $35 for an odd-sounding mantra that promised to take them deep inside themselves, beyond the grinding daily buzz of thought and circumstance. The experience made evangelists out of many—the initiated quickly spread the word about TM. Like early Christians, these fledgling TMers were single-minded, dropping their lives to work without pay or benefits to further their guru's cause.

For a man who had lived in a cave and served as a secretary, Maharishi had an eerie ability to connect with the media. Like benefactors, journalists seemed drawn to him and his quest. *Life* magazine proclaimed 1968 "The Year of the Guru," and featured Maharishi on the cover with groovy, hallucinogenic spirals framing his face. That was the year the Beatles—along with the actress Mia Farrow, the Scottish musician Donovan, and Mike Love of the Beach Boys—visited the Maharishi's ashram in Rishikesh. Suddenly, following a guru was the thing to do.

But something went wrong in Rishikesh, and that something is a matter of much debate. News accounts of the time reported that Maharishi made advances on Mia Farrow, and the Beatles stormed off. John Lennon wrote a song supposedly inspired by the incident, which he originally titled "Maharishi." He renamed it "Sexy Sadie," and the plaintive refrain asked, "What have you done? You made a fool of everyone."

The Beatles moved on but Maharishi's star continued to rise, and TM became increasingly entrenched in popular culture. By the mid-1970s, the Movement estimated that it had 600,000 practitioners, with celebrities such as actress Shirley MacLaine and football star Joe Namath continuing to promote Maharishi's techniques and vision. TM how-to books were a staple on the best-seller list, and at the time, the Movement estimates that an average of forty thousand people a month were learning the meditation practice. Maharishi had a preternatural gift for structuring his organization. Perhaps influenced by his years spent as a secretary to Guru Dev, Maharishi seemed to have a deep talent and ambition for self-promotion. He bought two Heidelberg presses and began printing elaborate pamphlets and books and mission statements. He sent them out to world leaders and set up hundreds of certified centers throughout the United States, Europe, and India. Later, best-selling author Adam Smith would describe TM as "the McDonald's of the meditation business."

Maharishi appeared on *The Tonight Show*; he spoke regularly to national audiences of thousands about the profound beauty of life, accessible through his trademarked mantras. Maharishi said that millions practiced Transcendental Meditation and a Gallup poll backed up his claim. A woman who spent time with Maharishi during those years would later write that Maharishi turned to her one day and asked her if she thought he should try to become the prime minister of India, or if he should continue to focus on his spiritual movement. He chose the Movement, but the question illustrated his grandiose ambition. (Decades later, that woman, who claimed she had spent years as Maharishi's mistress said that it wasn't his nonascetic proclivities that shocked her but his ambition.)

In January of 1972, Maharishi announced his "World Plan."

1. To develop the full potential of the individual
2. To improve governmental achievements
3. To realize the highest ideal of education
4. To solve the problems of crime, drug abuse, and all behavior that brings unhappiness to the family of man
5. To maximize the intelligent use of the environment
6. To bring fulfillment to the economic aspirations of individuals and society
7. To achieve the spiritual goals of mankind in this generation

A handpicked group of followers were chosen to establish 3,600 "World Plan Centers" around the world. These centers would be universities, one for every million of earth's 3.6 billion inhabitants, and the programs would offer the guru's special "consciousness-based" education, one that relied heavily on his life philosophy.

The next year, the guru launched the Maharishi International University; the first semester of classes took place in a crowded apartment in Santa Barbara, California. Around that time, Maharishi asked one of his devotees, Dr. Keith Wallace, a Harvard-trained neurophysiologist, to hunt for a college to buy that would become a permanent home for the university. On a tip, Dr. Wallace visited Fairfield, Iowa, home to Parsons College, a small Presbyterian school that had gone bankrupt.

By 1974, the TM Movement had a picturesque 272-acre campus. Maharishi declared that here they would build a "Unified Field Based Civilization." "This university is going to be a place like atomic reactors," said Maharishi at the time. "It's from there that the theories have been developed by the Unified Field."

Soon after, Maharishi assembled some of his most dedicated disciples in Seelisberg, Switzerland—then the TM global headquarters—and told them that he had a special announcement to make. A thrill went through the small group as they exchanged knowing glances—surely he was going to give them a mantra to make them Enlightened. Instead, he announced that he had bought a university in Iowa, and that he wanted them all to move there and become MBA students so that he could get more federal funding.

"You see," Maharishi reportedly told them, "the world is my checkerboard. And you are my pieces. And I can move you here and there to play the game right." He giggled and the group couldn't help but laugh too. World Peace, Maharishi told them, was waiting for everyone in Fairfield, Iowa.

CHAPTER TWO

The Hoffman Curse

My earliest memories of my dad are of being completely caught up in one of his wild stories. He would walk into my room and suddenly he'd be doing puppet theater—his hands would become neurotic animals, fighting over petty animal things. His voice would range from screechy to dopey and slow, and the mundane space around me would be transformed into some bizarre creature world. I would laugh until I couldn't see straight, trying not to pee in my pants. And then, just as quickly as he'd swooped in, he'd be gone. Tense, inaudible words exchanged with my mom, a door slamming, and everything was quiet again.

My dad was haunted by his history. Growing up, he told me about his parents and his grandparents, his aunts and uncles, his brother and sister the way you would a cautionary tale. To him, it was a Grimm's type of story, acted out by seemingly normal people who became witches and demons who then cast spells of addiction and abuse on their children. The past was a curse that he would forever try to outrun.

Dad was born in Cupertino, California, to high-school sweethearts from Eureka, Kansas. My grandfather Dave was a handsome but unknowable guy who held himself apart from everyone else.

He had a pompadour of blond hair and wore natty suits, looking like a Midwestern beatnik version of David Bowie. Dave's father, Louis, my dad's grandfather, was a cowboylike lifelong alcoholic who decided to quit drinking after his second wife killed herself at the age of eighty. Later in life I'd spend long afternoons with him in his backyard garden in Santa Cruz, talking about Pablo Neruda, while he smoked his Marlboro reds. But on his eighty-ninth birthday, he walked slowly down to the local grocer, bought a handle of booze, got drunk for the last time, and shot himself with a revolver in his little Craftsman cottage near the ocean.

For his part, Grandpa Dave acted impervious to it all: he could be cold, jealous, and, at times, grandiose. He pursued his self-interest diligently: he played the piano well, and had gigs in nightclubs and recording sessions and, even briefly, held a position at UC Santa Cruz teaching the history of jazz.

My grandma Bette was a distant and beautiful blonde, whose mother had been a spooky and cruel woman. Bette and Dave both drank, and their marriage didn't last long. When they split up, Dave disappeared from my dad's life, leaving him and his older brother Rip and his little sister Claudia to fend for themselves against Bette's second husband who had a taste for hard drinking and child beating. My father regaled me with stories of family suicides and violence; his history gave him the sense that life was almost too much to bear for a Hoffman.

My dad had been the smart, artistic one in his family, the one who seemed like he just might escape the family curse. He did a stint in the army, then went to UC Santa Cruz to study theater arts. His professors there told him that he had a gift for playwriting and encouraged him to apply to Yale and the University of Iowa Writers' Workshop. He proudly told me he was accepted to both.

But my dad couldn't seem to shake his past. He liked to drink, a lot, and when he did, he blacked out. Later he would tell me stories from those early days, when he would wake up to friends recounting his wild behavior—women chased around the street, trees chopped down.

He wanted to be different from the people he'd grown up with—more accomplished, more serious. But the Hoffman affliction loomed large. His brother had returned from Vietnam scarred and would later be arrested for armed robbery, spending years in federal prison. His beloved sister had run away from that darkness, and become a devout Jehovah's Witness. One day, Dad was walking down the street in Santa Cruz and he saw his father walking toward him. He stopped to say hello, but Dave walked past him refusing to meet his eyes. Dad couldn't think of what he'd done wrong. They never spoke again.

After her face-to-face encounter with Maharishi, my mother dropped out of college. All she cared about now was meditating and being around Maharishi. She worked long hours at the record shop in order to save money to travel to Europe and spend time with the guru. There she could learn how to teach meditation and help change the world. It all felt so good. She held group meditations in her home. Eventually, she saved enough to fly to Majorca, Spain, where Maharishi was holding teacher-training seminars. She spent six months there; these were her glory days, meditating for hours at a time, giddily talking consciousness with her new friends, all the while working in the kitchen to help pay her tuition. She wore flowing Indian skirts and laughed all the time. Everything seemed bright and hopeful and clear.

As much as she felt full of love for Maharishi, my mom didn't think of herself as a devotee. Not like some people. She noticed that there were course participants around her in Majorca who were utterly fixated on Maharishi. Sure, it made her day when he waved to her as he drove by in his limousine. But she didn't want to spend her life serving him. Yet there were men who rushed to meet his every need, girls who swooned in his presence, and this seemed a little much to her. She wanted his knowledge but she also wanted a normal life, albeit one filled with his brand of meditation and bliss.

After returning to America, she continued to deepen her practice by taking courses from the Transcendental Meditation Movement. In 1974, she went to a course on Maharishi's teachings at an old resort in San Jacinto, California. For a few days, meditators gathered to practice and watch videos of Maharishi's speeches. One afternoon she was sitting alone in the dining hall, drinking tea, when a shaggy-haired guy cleaning up the tables gave her a shy smile. As he lifted up a stack of plates, my mom warned him sweetly that it might be too heavy for him.

"I'm a heavy guy," he said, with a smile. My mom blushed. My dad was hooked. In those first days, they were inseparable. My mom fell hard for my dad's quirky humor and his puppy-dog eyes. My dad thought my mom was the most beautiful woman he'd ever seen—her shimmering honey-colored hair, her fluorescent blue eyes and delicate apple cheeks. The combination of her shyness and the offbeat way she looked at the world. Her innocence, to him, was remarkable.

My dad had learned TM the year before but it hadn't transformed his life the way it had for my mom. He loved the idea of not needing drugs or alcohol or his Marlboro reds to find happiness—but the truth was, he enjoyed all of them quite a bit. He'd come to the resort that weekend not out of devotion but out of a desperate hope to find a fresh start, to clean up his act.

He was twenty-six years old; Mom was twenty-four. When Mom asked him if he was a spiritual guy, he said, "No, I just try to be real." He was being witty but he felt a flash of shame. He knew he was screwed up. In her presence, Dad felt an overwhelming urge to erase his past and all his bad behaviors and be someone else entirely for this mesmerizing creature who was so in love with TM.

They were married within the year.

In their wedding photos, they look like they are on another planet where the air is made of love. They are staring at each other, arm in arm, sunflowers in their hands, soft, silly grins on their faces. In reality, my dad had started drinking even before the ceremony. As the day progressed, he felt pressure and anxiety. A voice inside him said, "I'll show her who I really am." He wanted to push back against the idea of the man my mom wanted him to be. By the time they got home, he was barely conscious, yelling at her as she climbed onto a chair in the corner to hide from his ranting. This became the pattern of their marriage—him hiding his addictions and his darkness, and then, when he inevitably succumbed, terrifying her with them. Meanwhile, she dutifully went through the motions of being a wife and mother, using meditation to soften the harshness of her new out-of-control adult life.

My brother was born the next year, in 1975, in Boulder. I came along two years after that, in 1977, in Iowa City, Iowa, where my father was finishing his master's degree at the Iowa Writers' Workshop. By then, my father had stopped meditating with my mom and started going out more and more to drink with his friends. On the other side of the world, far from the increasingly disordered life of my parents, Maharishi was celebrating victory.

An estimated eight million people had learned his trademarked form of meditation and the guru christened 1977 "The Year of Ideal Society."

We ended up in Manhattan at Ninety-Seventh Street and West End Avenue, a neighborhood that my mother, who had grown up in the quiet suburbs of Princeton, viewed as a war zone. It was 1980 and our once-stately apartment building was surrounded by SROs (single-room occupancy apartments, inhabited mainly by people Mom called "bums"). I would peer down from our sixth-floor window to watch these characters holding bottles in paper bags as they staggered in and out of lobbies. The streets below us seemed wild—strewn with garbage and trash, filled with taxi tires squealing, buses honking, people jostling and yelling.

Before we moved in, our apartment had belonged to an elderly Jewish couple who had died there after occupying the place for half a century. We'd gotten the apartment after my parents had struck a deal with their son—we would sort through and discard all their old stuff, which he had no interest in. What I remember most was the treasure trove of postcards, hundreds of postcards, sent from places like Niagara Falls and Yosemite, written in indecipherable handwriting with dates from the turn of the century. Something about those postcards felt familiar, like adventures that I had been on and forgotten. Waterfalls, statues, mountains—I felt like they were a record of our journeys before we had landed here on the Upper West Side.

As far as my mother was concerned, the only things that held back the chaos of the world were the thick glass windows and yellowing plaster walls of our apartment—and her. She stood over us like a protective shield, trying to keep the pandemonium at bay.

My parents had found this apartment as soon as we'd moved to New York. We'd moved three times in the last two years since my dad had finished his master's degree. We'd lived in Baton Rouge and St. Louis and Alexandria, Virginia, chasing writing work for Dad. But New York was where he wanted to pursue his dream, which was to write plays that lots of people would see.

Dad had written and directed one play that appeared in a place that he called "off-off" Broadway, and I had wanted to go, but he said it wasn't for kids. The only evidence I had of its existence was the old pieces of painted cardboard sets he'd brought home from the show—brightly colored trees and flowers that became part of the piecemeal furnishings in our large dining room. I'd never been to a play so I didn't really know what theater was, despite the presence of the "theater people" who would come through town and stay with us—the puppeteers from Santa Cruz, the mime from France, the young actress who'd lived in the maid's room at the back of the apartment for months and helped us pay our rent. I loved the energy of my father's world, the uneasy excitement that seemed to surround him and his friends. I never knew what would happen—I would be hurled onto somebody's shoulders; a bag of Chinese food would appear filled with fish heads; a beautiful actress—somebody's girlfriend—would start singing songs from *Annie* to me.

Mom was always off to the side busy with the obligations of being an adult—or else she was meditating. I remember her as a blur of dutiful activity: cleaning, or cooking us zucchini bread and tofu, or huddled in a corner having hushed phone conversations. I would watch as she pulled the phone into the kitchen pantry to whisper to her friends or to her mother, or as she sat at the dining room table with a piece of graph paper and a pen, making long lists of items with numbers next to them in neat, tiny handwriting.

Through it all, meditation was always our touchstone, the organizing principal of our day. In the morning when we woke up, we
would tiptoe into my mom's bedroom, where she would be sitting
propped up against the wall, her eyes closed, my dad snoring beside
her. In the evening, she'd shut herself in the living room for over an
hour while we played quietly. Once Stacey finally learned his Word
of Wisdom, we would do our own meditation together, playing
alongside each other without speaking for the allotted five minutes.
But there was also an awkward furtiveness to our practice. We would
have to leave early from a friend's house or make excuses at school
for why Mom couldn't do anything for long stretches in the morning
and again in the afternoon. Meditation was important to us, but it
also felt like a family secret. We didn't talk about it to outsiders.

One morning, not long after I turned five, I shuffled from my bedroom to the dining room to eat breakfast and squealed with excitement when I saw Dad sitting at the table, reading the paper and
drinking his coffee. We rarely saw him these days—he seemed to
be on a very different schedule from the rest of us. He held Mom's
hand and made funny little whispered jokes about us to her as we
all ate buckwheat pancakes. She laughed, but I felt like her eyes
were looking everywhere but at him, almost as if she was afraid. I
stared at her, trying to figure out what was going on. But before I
could get too concerned, Dad leaped up from the table with excitement.

We were going to go to a kind of museum, he said, his voice
cartoony and thrilled. A special museum we'd never been to and it
was better than a museum—it was a castle! As Mom got us dressed,
Dad stood in the doorway of our room and told us about how
amazing this place called the Cloisters was—full of old stuff from

kings and queens from a long time ago, including a tapestry with a unicorn. A unicorn! I couldn't wait.

I loved the feeling as we walked down the street together, the four of us, to the bus. Stacey was holding Dad's hand and talking a mile a minute about the knives and the armor we were going to see. But on the bus, Dad stopped talking. It was a long ride uptown, and Dad's face seemed to be getting tighter and tighter. Mom stopped talking too and Stacey and I whispered to ourselves, trying to ignore them and imagine the wonders we were about to see.

It seemed like hours later when we emerged from the bus and into the chilly spring sunshine. Dad wasn't holding Stacey's hand anymore. He was walking ahead of us, beads of sweat running down his forehead and the back of his neck. He stopped and turned to Mom, grabbing her arm hard and whispering in her ear. She said something, sad and sharp. And then he was gone.

"Where's he going?" I asked.

"He needs a drink," Mom said flatly, looking around this neighborhood that was utterly foreign to us. Her blue eyes were full of tears as she led us over to a bench. Her long hair covered her face—she was thirty-one years old then but people always asked her if she was our babysitter because she looked so young. From where we were sitting I could see the turrets of the castle and I tried to go back to thinking about the unicorn and what it would look like. After a while, Stacey asked when we were going to the castle, and Mom's voice broke as she answered, "We have no money." Her body started to shudder and shake as she began crying, hard. I held her hand. Stacey stared off into space, resting his cheek on her shoulder. After what felt like forever, a man stopped in front of the bench and asked her what was wrong. Mom said we'd been left there and we had no money to get home. He gave her a few dollars. Avoiding his eyes, she thanked him and grabbed our hands. We marched back to the bus stop, both of us turning our heads to get a last glance at the regal stones of the castle.

As spring turned to summer, things got worse. During this time, I mostly remember a continual feeling of dread. I was little but observant enough to know that our family was teetering on the edge of chaos. One night after all the lights were out, I lay wide awake, certain there was a tiger in my closet. Every once in a while he seemed to appear, glimmering and orange, his fur vibrating with a hallucinatory aliveness. I was squinting to see him when I heard the front door slam shut. Dad was home. I closed my eyes. I wasn't supposed to be awake. I heard his footsteps creak down the hall and the door of their bedroom squeak open. Then I heard my parents' voices getting louder and louder as they came into the hallway. Dad was screaming at Mom. He wanted his dinner. Every night Mom left an extra serving in the oven for Dad, but for months now, I had watched her throw the food away in the morning, untouched.

In his bed next to me, I heard Stacey roll over, his covers rustling. I looked over the edge of my blankets, and saw him sitting up. "Daaaaad," he called out. Our parents stopped talking. "Daaaad," Stacey pleaded. My heart was beating fast. Dad appeared in the doorway of our bedroom, swaying from side to side. Stacey looked up at him and gave him a tentative smile and in a funny voice—a voice just like Dad used with our stuffed animals—he said, "Can you pipe down, buster?"

In an instant, Dad had moved from the doorway to Stacey's bed and lifted him up in the air. My mom let out a choking sound. Stacey wiggled his legs, clad in pajamas covered in spaceships.

"Dooooon't," Stacey cried—but Dad wasn't listening to him. He wasn't saying a word as he dragged Stacey out of the room and into the hall toward the bathroom. I climbed out and ran after them. In the bathroom, my mom was standing in the doorway, moaning. Dad was holding Stacey over the sink, trying to pin his arms down. Stacey was wriggling like a fish, trying to escape from my father's grip.

"I'm going to wash your mouth out with soap," Dad said, his voice flat and empty. "You can never fucking talk to me like that." I watched Stacey try to wrench his face away from the faucet. The light from the street came through the little window near the toilet and cast a ghostly blue over everything. With one last contortion, Stacey managed to free himself and run out of the room, my mom following him, tears streaming down her face.

My dad was bent over the sink, panting. He seemed like a different person, one I had never seen before. I stood there in my long flowery flannel nightgown as he turned on the old faucet with a squeak and splashed water on his sweaty face, droplets coating his grizzled brown beard. When he looked in the mirror and saw me there, staring at him, his eyes welled up. And then he slammed the door in my face. Standing in the long dark hallway, looking at that closed door, I tried to conjure up my mantra, something powerful to make him stop hating us.

A week later, from out of the blue, the family that lived in the apartment above ours offered my mom a chance to spend a weekend at their place in the country. She jumped on it, discreetly packing our bags the night before we were to leave, while Dad was gone. The next morning, she hustled us out the door while Dad was still asleep. We tiptoed down the long hallway, careful not to make a sound. Not waking up Dad was now an unspoken rule in our home, as strictly observed as not interrupting Mom during her meditation.

The dark, garbage-strewn steps of the subway were already baking in the summer heat as the three of us descended to the platform to catch a subway to Penn Station.

"Why isn't Dad coming?" I asked. Stacey glared at me. He had just had his seventh birthday and it felt like every chance he got, he wanted to remind me that, at five, I was a total moron. I blushed, but I couldn't figure out what I had done wrong. Mom looked straight ahead, shouldering our family tote bag. "He had to work," she said as she moved us through the turnstile. I pulled my Snoopy doll in close, burying my mouth in his matted gray fur and thought about how this was good news. I knew he needed work, and it was something that my mom wanted him to do more. Also, he had promised to take me to *Annie* that week, and I selfishly hoped no one was going to mess that up.

On the train, I sat next to the window, pressing my face against the glass, watching as the slow streaks of buildings, gray and brown, turned into longer, blurry stretches of green. I thought about Dad and how sad he must be to not be coming with us. Still, I liked how relaxed Mom seemed without him. Stacey too seemed relieved. He had folded down his tray table and was drawing a big dinosaur, with Mom laughing at the funny little hands he'd drawn on the creature. We didn't talk about Dad after what had happened in the bathroom. He felt like a black hole in our lives—dangerous and unknown.

When we arrived at our neighbor's house in Pennsylvania, I began to feel a sense of relief too. The couple wasn't so close with my parents, but they had a boy and girl who were five and seven, and the four of us often played together in our building. For me, though, the big attraction was the woods. They made me feel like I was inside one of my storybooks—everything was so alive and green, the smell of pine intoxicating, and I couldn't wait to make friends with all the animals that lived there.

In the short span of that weekend, I felt like we experienced a whole summer. In Manhattan, I couldn't do anything outside our apartment without my hand firmly gripped by my mother's. But at this small wooden cabin, surrounded by rolling acres of pine trees and fields of wild strawberries, she had scanned the backyard and assured herself that there were no bad guys in sight. The moment she let go of my hand I exploded into the fields, racing for hours after my brother and our friends. All I felt was air, pumping through my lungs and into my head.

I don't remember eating or sleeping during that entire trip—although, of course, I must have. Still, my memory of it is of spending every second playing hide-and-seek. I considered myself a hide-and-seek mastermind—or maybe even something greater than that, maybe I had special powers that actually allowed me to disappear? I was slight and small for my age so I could tuck myself into the tiniest spots, squeezing into a log pile or standing stick straight behind a narrow tree. I loved watching the others race around, yelling and searching, while I stood frozen, relishing having a secret all my own. I'd use my mantra to quiet my body, imagining that my stillness made me invisible.

Mom seemed like she took up more space here, away from the city, away from Dad and his moods. She laughed with our neighbors in the little kitchen as she helped slice vegetables. She stretched out on the patio with her hands flopped at her side, totally at rest. She smiled indulgently as we returned from the woods, covered in mud, and listened patiently to our war stories. I basked in her happiness. I thought she was so beautiful when she was happy—she looked like a kid with her eyes sparkling and her little mouth spread open in an easy smile.

On our last day there, we took a group hike in the woods, along a path next to a sparkling lake. I was walking slowly, behind everyone else, stopping often to search for a magic pebble, like the one in the book Mom would read to me sometimes. Stacey was in front, with a stick in his hand, which he used to trace a long line in the dirt on the path. We were both in inspection mode—looking for something special to take back to the city and show Dad, something that would give us a great story we could tell him.

When I heard Stacey shout, I thought maybe he'd found a snake, which I instantly decided would be the most exciting and dangerous story that we could return with. Instead, it was a small box turtle with a greenish-brown shell and little glints of orange on his belly. Stacey bent down and picked him up from the leafy patch. I could hardly breathe from excitement, watching all his tiny little turtle toes as he made his way up Stacey's pale arm. I felt a surge of jealousy that this turtle would be only Stacey's story to share. I pushed in closer. "But what will he eat?" Mom asked, and I knew then that the turtle was coming home with us. We named him Myrtle the Turtle, snickering at the storybook rhyme—Dad would love it. We put him in an empty tissue box filled with bits of grass and potato bugs. Stacey carefully balanced the box on his lap the whole way back to the city.

Racing up to our apartment I was wheezing with emotion, giggling at the very thought of how my dad would animate Myrtle's grumpy mouth. Stacey's lips were moving as he rehearsed what he was going to say when we presented Dad with the little cardboard den with Myrtle inside.

Downstairs in the lobby, Mom had stopped in the stairwell and I could hear her talking to our landlord, a potbellied man whose gray whiskers always looked wet, and who glared whenever we walked past. I heard him say a word, loud and hard—"Eviction"—and I wondered what it meant. I couldn't hear my mom very well, she was murmuring to him politely, and a minute later she was trudging up the stairs, her face stiff as she fished around in her canvas bag for the keys. "Your dad hasn't paid the rent in months," she said quietly. I didn't say anything. I didn't want to distract from the excitement of Myrtle's homecoming, and my trip to see *Annie*.

Mom shoved open the thick front door and we raced past her into the old white-tiled kitchen, but it was empty, so we pushed on through the big wood swinging doors into the living room, and then the dining room. Light streamed in the windows from the afternoon sun. No sign of Dad anywhere. But on the long dining room table I saw a yellow lined notepad, with his big, sprawling, all-capital letter handwriting on it. "LIZ." That, I could read. Next to it was a small pile of money. I felt something sick in my stomach. Mom came through the kitchen doors; she seemed to be moving in slow motion as she walked over to the table and wilted into a chair. Stacey had taken one look at the note and disappeared down the hall, quietly surveying the rest of the rooms in the apartment.

Dad was gone.

Stacey came back from the bedroom and sank onto the couch, staring intently down at his cardboard turtle cage. I stood next to Mom's chair, knowing that I shouldn't say a word. I could feel sadness steaming off her like smoke. I tried to think back to the time before we left for the woods. What had I done to make Dad go away?

I figured Dad must have been sad that we'd left him. Maybe I

CHAPTER THREE

Stranger in a Strange Land

It was my third kindergarten. My third first day of school. My third home in my third state in less than a year. My brother and I got ready quietly, tiptoeing around while my mom meditated in the tiny upstairs room of our new home in Fairfield, Iowa. We'd been there only a few weeks, the winter temperature had yet to rise above zero, and the house was freezing. It seemed like the window frames weren't attached to the walls—cold air came gusting through every crack. So the day before, Mom and a few of her new friends had bought a roll of plastic, and spent the afternoon duct-taping the edges of the clear material over each window. Now the morning light in the living room radiated through the plastic, bordered by dark swaths of tape. It felt as if we were in a fish tank. When I pressed my face against the window near the door, I could see the snow swirling down in smoky puffs, piling up in the street in thick white banks. I hoped maybe the snow would bury us in and I wouldn't have to go to school.

Stacey and I had just finished practicing our Word of Wisdom. We did it together every morning and every afternoon, for five minutes at a time. With my dad taking off and us moving all the time, our meditation had become the only consistent part of our day. Mom liked her privacy when she meditated, so Stacey and I did it together, silently wandering around the house, staring out the window, and coloring in our coloring books.

The silence continued even after our five minutes were over, the house hushed as we went about making our breakfast. There was nothing worse than Mom coming out of her meditation, crazy eyed, to yell at us for disrupting her quiet time.

Stacey and I hadn't been talking much anyway these days. I pulled a bag of whole wheat bread out of the refrigerator and Stacey snatched it away before I could take a slice. Somewhere in the chaos of moving and new homes and new schools, our tight bond had eroded. Stacey rarely wanted to play or draw with me anymore. He'd hardened against me, taking every opportunity to let me know how lame and babyish I was. I could tell that everything about me disgusted him—my sucked-on stuffed animals, my weepy questions about Dad. Stacey liked things to be just so—his G.I. Joe figures lined up tightly on the shelf, his brown shirt worn with his brown pants. Everything had gone topsy-turvy, and Stacey, in an effort to create a clean line, had located me as the source of the problem.

After we got the letter from Dad and the eviction notice, Mom had packed up all our belongings. Soon after, a group of her friends cheerfully carried the boxes into a giant truck waiting outside our building. We went for a short time to my grandfather's house in Princeton, but my mom and her stepmother barely spoke to each other. My mom had always felt like her stepmother viewed her as an irritant and during our stay Mom got the sense that she didn't like the idea of her, a single mother mooching off her husband. On our last day, my grandfather quietly played Legos with us and then waved good-bye.

From there, we drove in a rental truck to Green Cove Springs, Florida, to stay with my grandmother. Despite the drama of her childhood, my mom had always stayed in touch with her mother, writing letters about her TM retreats, and dutifully reporting our childhood milestones. When my father took off, Denny was my mom's first phone call. She was all she had at that point.

My grandmother lived in a little cottage—with three small bedrooms and a sandy backyard—with her ninety-four-year-old mother, my great-grandmother, Tess. Tess spent most of the day lying in her bed in the front bedroom, where she read books and prayed, while nibbling little chocolate mints that she kept close by. The smell of the sulfur springs for which the town was named infused the house.

When she thought we were asleep, my mother frequently closed herself off in the tiny bedroom at the back of the house and cried.

One hot afternoon, Stacey and I were waiting in the backseat of my grandmother's car and fighting over a little camera. Stacey pushed me and accidentally hit my face, and my nose started spurting blood. I screamed hysterically. I had never seen that much blood, let alone from my own body. I knew it was an accident—I had been hitting Stacey too—but I was terrified that I would bleed to death. Mom dragged Stacey into the house, shouting at him in a wild, mean voice. After that, every time he shoved me, Mom threatened to make Stacey wash the toilet, which made his animosity toward me grow exponentially. Everything about our circumstances—and family—felt broken.

Soon after our arrival in Florida, and at the urging of her friends from the TM Movement, Mom flew to Fairfield, Iowa, and stayed there for a week. When she returned, she told us she'd found a home for us and even a job, making handcrafted picture frames for a local artist. Fairfield, she told us, was an extraordinary place where lots of people meditated—adults and children. The idea of moving to Iowa thrilled me. I imagined a life somewhere between *Little House on the Prairie* and *Charlotte's Web*. Barnyard animals would dance, I would roll through the meadows, and learn to ride a bike, and, at long last, I would be allowed to go out of the house alone.

More than all of that, I relished the idea that I might finally have friends who also meditated twice a day, and who would understand what it was like to have a hidden life inside your head.

But when I peered out the window as the plane descended into the Burlington, Iowa, airport, the view was cold and bleak. Through the frosted oval, I saw a dull checkerboard of brown fields and farmhouses. Plumes of smoke from factories rose up in the air. Other than that, it was absolutely still. I gazed intently down at this sad-looking ant-farm world. It didn't look anything like the picture of Iowa I'd had in my mind—where were the bright green fields, the picket fences, the chorus line of singing farm animals?

The tiny plane shuddered onto the runway, snow swirling around it. I held Mom's hand tight as we made our way off the plane and into the dingy airport. She seemed agitated and upset and I pushed my head against her leg, hoping to distract her. It was below zero. In the rush to pack everything and say good-bye to her mother, she had forgotten to pack a coat for herself. The wind was blowing, and the airport terminal was little more than a shed. Standing next to her, looking around at this dull frozen tundra, I felt petrified, tired, and disappointed. What were we doing here?

Inside, my mom's college friend Jeff was waiting for her. He offered her his coat, and we packed the few bags we had into his VW station wagon, then piled into the backseat. The midafternoon sun hit the stretches of small hillsides along the road as we drove toward Fairfield. Though I'd been born in Iowa, while my dad was in graduate school, it looked entirely exotic to me. I had never seen a sky so big—it went on forever, in every direction. The land was gentle and rolling, stretching out into endless fallow fields.

Arriving in Fairfield, we drove along a large winding boulevard, lined on both sides with large Victorian and Craftsman houses. Large oak trees towered over the homes and gray snowbanks bordered the road. We drove to the north side of town, where the campus was situated. There, the houses got smaller—humble wood-frame homes, paint peeling, with sagging porches and ripped screen doors. We drove up to the house that we'd be renting. It looked like it was out of a fairy tale, but not in the way I might have hoped. Perched on a busy corner, the Pepto-Bismol-pink house seemed to be tilting to the side, almost as if it were going to fall into the large, snow-covered vacant lot next door. "We're here!" Mom said cheerfully. I wished that we could magically go back to our sun-filled apartment on the Upper West Side.

That first morning, getting ready for kindergarten, I felt my stomach turn at the thought of a whole new set of kids to contend with, all those eyes staring at me. In New York I'd had lots of friends and loved school. But after my dad left and then the tumult of Florida, I felt timid. If Stacey's view of me was accurate, I was a weakling loser. I tried to eat some of my cashew-buttered toast, but I couldn't quite get it down. Mom came downstairs from her meditation and hustled us into our hand-me-down snow pants and winter coats.

When she'd come to Fairfield, alone, on her scouting trip, she'd met an older guy, who had recently immigrated from Europe, named Boris, who'd promised her a good salary crafting heart-shaped ceramic frames that he was going to sell to bookstores around the country. Boris had also offered to rent her a two-bedroom house. She'd come back and boasted to us about it—we'd have our own home, with a yard. But when we arrived in Iowa, Boris put Mom in a basement workstation and paid her less than minimum wage. Meanwhile, our house was falling apart and, despite it being advertised as furnished, all we had were a few pieces of old foam to sleep on. Within days of arrival, Mom put together a budget on the back of an envelope and realized that we wouldn't break even. She applied for food stamps.

This also meant that we couldn't afford to go to the private school, the Maharishi School of the Age of Enlightenment, as we'd originally planned. I had been so excited to meet other kids who also had their own Word of Wisdom, but now I just watched them from the window as they ambled home in the afternoon, an hour after public school let out. The Maharishi school kids wore spiffy uniforms—navy jumpers and sweaters, red ties and bows, crisp white shirts. But for us, the combined $3,000 annual tuition was out of the question.

Life had felt turbulent moving from New York to Florida, but, here in Iowa, I felt poor for the first time. We had been through winter in New York but nothing compared to what happened outside our little home on the prairie. The snow seemed to just tumble down out of the sky and when you walked outside your whole body stung from the cold. Mom took us to the local Goodwill store near the hospital. For Stacey, she found an army green down coat with a few holes that had been patched with duct tape. For me, she found an ugly short gray jacket with pink stripes. I gazed at the floor as she took them to the register, a look of resolution on her face. I knew I couldn't say anything, but I hated the coat, and

I hated the feeling of being stuffed into someone else's cast-offs. The stains were not mine. Worse, I was scared that someone would recognize it and shout out at me that I was wearing their coat.

My mother was determined to make things better for us. But it seemed to me that she placed all of her hopes for doing this on what she called "the Flying Course." Learning to fly, she was sure, would turn things around for us. She told us about an advanced form of meditation that Maharishi had revealed—drawing from ancient Vedic scripture—that allowed you to levitate and hover in the air.

Looking back now, I see that flying for my mom was an enchanted escape hatch from the chaos that our life had become. She believed that by practicing Maharishi's advanced techniques she would change her consciousness and garner the elusive "Nature Support" that Maharishi said came from going deeper and deeper into the Unified Field. "Nature Support," my mother thought, would mean more money, more stability, more happiness for our family. And she truly believed that by learning this technique she would become Enlightened—just like Maharishi. When we asked what she meant by Enlightenment, she said that it was when you were unconditionally happy and nature supported you and the universe gave you everything you wanted. Nature Support sounded to me like a genie from my *The Arabian Nights* storybook, a powerful personality that could grant my every wish.

I didn't question that this felt like a priority over living in a place where she could've had real career opportunities—or why our most urgent financial wish was to pay for the Flying Course. I understood implicitly then that Mom was pursuing change through the only means she truly believed in: Maharishi and his meditation.

"Do your program to support spontaneous right action and glean the support of nature!" Maharishi said. To Mom, this was as good as gold. I wanted it for her, for all of us. The only thing was, we needed Nature Support in order to get Nature Support: Mom didn't have the thousands of dollars in tuition that it cost to learn to fly. So we bided our time, waiting for some kind of miracle to happen.

The cold outside hit our Florida-tanned faces as we walked stiffly, like bedraggled snowmen, through the snow bluffs for our first day at Lincoln Elementary, a small public school on the north end of town. As I walked into the low-slung brick building, Mrs. Brush, a stout woman with hair growing out of her moles greeted me with hardened eyes. She asked where I had lived and I told her Florida and before that New York. She took a quick look at my mother— with her long silky hair and flowing skirt—and knew what I didn't know yet: I was an outsider, an invader.

"Why don't we have Ananda help you put your coat away," Mrs. Brush said curtly, drawing out Ananda's name with a drawl. Ananda appeared out of the crowd of Kristis, Shanes, and Scotts. She had sparkly brown eyes and a gap-toothed smile. My stained coat felt as if it would suffocate me as I looked around the room. I slid it off and handed it to Ananda, who quietly walked me over to the coat cubbies. The room smelled like Lysol and everyone was staring at me, in my favorite calico prairie dress and with my hair in two long blond braids.

"Are you a 'ru?" Ananda asked.

"A what?"

"A 'ru, a guru. A meditator?"

"Yeah," I said, my eyes flicking over to the small tables where the rest of the kids were sitting. "My mom meditates. She came here to learn to fly."

Ananda was already looking away from me, moving back toward the rest of the kids. "Don't tell anyone that," she said softly.

And then I was alone.

At lunchtime, I followed my classmates into the large cafeteria and found a place near Ananda, who mostly ignored me. She talked instead to a pretty blond girl with tight curls and pierced ears named Jamie. Everyone opened their lunchboxes, each one festooned with some cartoon superhero. I pulled out a brown paper bag, on which my mom had written my name in marker and drawn a little heart. I placed a bagel sandwich with cheese and tomato, a natural foods juice box, a few carrot sticks, and a little malted carob ball on the table in front of me. I looked up and saw that all the kids around me were staring.

"What's wrong with your bread?" one kid asked. I stared at the bagel.

"Not sure. It's a bagel?" I replied quietly.

"It has a hole in it," the kid replied.

"It's supposed to," I shot back, sensing an insult coming. Bagels were one of my favorite foods—we had eaten them all the time when we lived in New York. Now, my mom bought us frozen Lender's bagels for our sandwiches. I watched the kids around me giving each other looks, retreating from any future friendship. Jamie turned perkily toward me and asked sweetly, "Does your mom fly?"

Ananda picked at her sandwich.

"Um, no." I said. But then I couldn't resist telling the exciting truth. "Not yet."

From then on, I was marked. Stacey and I walked home from

school in silence, deflated after that first day. We had bonded over the idea of being with other kids who were like us, kids whose parents also disappeared for long stretches of the day. Instead, we were now surrounded by people who knew about this secret world—and thought we were crazy.

At home, we tried to be cheerful about school so that Mom wouldn't be too sad about our life here. So far, despite the weather and our financial struggles, she'd been happier in Iowa than she had been at my grandmother's house in boggy Florida. That night, for our nightly ritual of reading, we curled around her on the piece of foam that she was using for her bed. A friend of hers back in New York who had a degree in early childhood education had told her offhandedly that the single most important thing one could do for their children was read to them. My mom had embraced this truism with a vengeance and we very quickly moved from reading picture books to longer novels like *A Wrinkle in Time* or the Narnia books. In Florida, I had been the only kid in my kindergarten class who could read on my own—I'd be sent to the back of the room to read by myself while the other kids worked on phonics. It was a point of private pride for me as a kid that my family loved books, and consequently, I was a great reader—I soon realized this was more socially acceptable to brag about than meditating.

That first year in Iowa, Mom read the entire *Lord of the Rings* trilogy to us. Coming home each day from my rough-and-tumble school, it was what I looked forward to the most. After Mom finished her meditation, and after we cleaned up our dinner plates, we would put our pajamas on and climb onto Mom's foam bed. I'd snuggle up to her warm chest, smell the apple-y clean freshness of her hair, and disappear into the sound of her soft voice as she read to us about Frodo and Bilbo Baggins, Gollum and Gandalf.

Gandalf, in fact, was our safe word. Even though we were in a small idyllic town in the Midwest, my mom's fears of us being kidnapped—or worse—were not abated. She told us that first night that if anyone came to pick us up from school, they had to say Gandalf. I loved the idea of some mysterious person arriving at school, to whisk us away while invoking the enchantment of Middle Earth here in the drab Midwest. But it never happened.

Mom's fears of dark doings didn't seem completely ungrounded; danger did seem to loom everywhere in Iowa. Inside the entrance to Lincoln, the school principal had hung a large wooden paddle and on the first day I was told that misbehavior—such as talking back—would result in public paddlings. A large hardscrabble family lived next door to us; their constant screams and yells echoed often through our hushed, incense-filled home, occasionally ending in the wail of a police siren. The father would show up at recess and shake the chain-link fence and yell at his kids for being in school, mocking them for their lack of freedom. A few months later, Mom sat us down and told us that this man had "fallen asleep" on the nearby railroad tracks and died. Even then I had a feeling he'd done it on purpose.

One day, Stacey came home from school crying, his face scratched up. A group of townie kids had invited him over to play but when he arrived they'd thrown rocks at him, screaming, "Go home, guru!" over and over. My mother was hysterical when she saw what had happened to her son.

It felt as if we had our noses pressed up against the glass of everything we wanted. Our life felt more tenuous than ever—we were in a brutally cold place where we were outsiders, both from the local Iowans and the Movement we were supposed to take part in.

CHAPTER FOUR

Levitation

A few months after we'd moved to Fairfield, Mom said that Maharishi had put out a call to his followers all over the world to come for something called the Taste of Utopia, where everyone would meditate together for the month of December. Waiting for my mom to end her shift at the health food store where she now worked, I watched streams of customers pour in, stomping their snowy shoes in the doorway, and chattering away in languages I had never heard. Tall, blond European women in fur coats and Indian men in white robes under down jackets filled the aisles. The owner had ordered all sorts of strange foods to satisfy his new global market. I would wander around and marvel at the exotic wares—sticky balls of syrupy Indian dough, Swedish cough drops, goat's milk, crumbly bars of halvah. At the checkout counter, Mom did the math on a calculator, because, although there were three lines, there was only one cash register. She looked harried as she rang up the groceries on her little keypad.

Those first few months in Fairfield I felt like I was holding my breath, waiting for winter to end and the Taste of Utopia to come. You could see the effects of Maharishi's call to Iowa everywhere in Fairfield. The whole town seemed to be bracing for the Taste of Utopia course and Maharishi's arrival in December. Mom said that all the new people coming in would change everything that was wrong with our life in Fairfield—with the population suddenly exploding there would be more and better work for her. I hoped so. In the time since we'd moved there, I had become keenly aware of money. I was sure that if we just had more of it, Mom would be happy. Or happier. Mom said we were poor now and I felt that our poorness showed all over me.

Mom took on a flurry of part-time jobs in addition to her job at the health food store—working for the lesbian couple across the street, designing stuffed animals, painting an inspirational Christian art poster, and waiting tables at the health food diner near the railroad tracks. It felt like we hardly ever saw her. Though I almost never thought consciously of my dad, it pained me to be away from my mother for even a few hours.

When she was home, I battled Stacey and the endless pile of bills for her attention. My mom's recognition felt like armor from the chaos of the world. She was a talented artist and she spent hours designing miniature furnishings for the battered dollhouse a neighbor had given me. She used a tiny brush to paint the little cups and saucers that she had fashioned out of salt dough. She stretched out beside me on the floor and helped me arrange the itty-bitty fruits and vegetables she had made on the model table. She egged me on as I made up dollhouse operas. "You're such an unusual kid, Claire-beaux," she would say. It made me feel totally at home. I held that idea close—I wasn't an outcast like they said at school. Some weirdo guru. I was unusual.

When spring came, I begged my mom to let me throw away my shitty old coat. By next winter, there'd be World Peace and we would be able to afford a new one. My mom laughed and said, "Yes." We knew change was coming.

More and more, my mom seemed to have a whirlwind of single mom friends who were in and out of the house. Courtenay, a petite blonde from Connecticut, had moved to Fairfield the year before us. Like mom, she had done TM in the '70s, and when she got her divorce, the Maharishi community seemed like the safest place to go. Courtenay was effervescent and bold, a perfect counterbalance to my mom, who could be shy and introspective. She and Mom would sit at our small kitchen table on the weekends and talk for what seemed like hours—about men, meditation, money. I wished sometimes they would stop saying so many bad things about the opposite sex. Stacey was often the only boy around and I worried that he might feel bad. We'd linger around them until they pushed us to go outside and play. Then we'd descend into the backyard, with its carpet of dead leaves. Stacey would boss Courtenay's two daughters and me around as he organized elaborate games of fantasy warfare.

Without much explanation, Jeff, my mom's former college boyfriend, became her new, for-real boyfriend. Jeff shared an apartment with a friend, but almost every night he came to our house with Mom after they'd meditated at the Golden Domes. The domes were the two huge oval-shaped buildings that had recently been built on campus where people practiced the flying technique. There was a dome for men and a dome for women. I had only seen them from the outside during our evening walks. They looked like giant gleaming golden spaceships with funny little curved windows along the perimeter. I had never seen anything like it and had always wanted to go in.

Jeff played with us as Mom cooked barbecued tofu and veggies in the small kitchen. His hair fell in a fluffy, wavy frame around his face. His voice was big and loud and booming, and when he walked around town, everyone seemed to want to talk to him.

With Jeff, I felt like the center of attention. He would pull my braids and tease me for being little or skinny or for being moody and distant. He seemed to notice my quiet acts of rebellion that had, until then, mostly gone unnoticed. He wore soft linen-y shirts and a strand of wooden rudraksha beads. He had tortoiseshell glasses and teeth that seemed to be at all angles. But I thought he was so handsome.

What I really loved was the way he made my mom happy. She always seemed to be blushing and laughing in his presence, girlishly light and excited. He wandered around the apartment, stooping under the low ceilings, exuding good cheer as he kissed Mom on the cheek and complimented her. He was a full foot taller than she was, and he always seemed to be leaning in toward her, curling his long arms around her. The things that usually bothered her barely seemed to register when he was around—Stacey blasting Mötley Crüe or me whining about not having a Strawberry Shortcake doll—she took it all in an easy stride.

I decided that I didn't really miss my dad anymore. I felt embarrassed when people asked about him. Sometimes when I fell down and hurt myself or got teased in school, I longed for him or at least the vague memory of his scratchy beard, but now that we had Jeff, I hoped he would be our new dad.

Jeff had just gotten his master's degree from Maharishi International University. He'd quit his job as a lab technician at the university where he had done experiments proving that TM did all sorts of wonderful things for the brain. Jeff had spent the last few years on Purusha. Jeff explained to me that Purusha was a group of men who lived a celibate lifestyle, in the hopes of becoming Enlightened quickly, and who meditated and worked full-time for Maharishi. You didn't get paid though, and so Jeff had left. He had said he'd gotten tired of being poor but now he didn't have a job. He and Mom would joke together about how broke they both were.

There was so little that we could afford to do that first year. I mostly remember us walking. We would walk together in the evening after dinner and on the weekends. "Let's go for a Walk and Talk," Mom would say gamely, when she finished meditating. Walk and Talk was the name Maharishi had given to the time slots in between long meditation sessions during the courses that Mom and Jeff had both taken in Spain and Italy, when they were in their twenties and living from meditation course to meditation course. Then, they would talk for hours about their experiences in meditating and their consciousness and Maharishi's philosophy. None of that interested me very much, though it seemed like Mom and Jeff could talk about Maharishi and their consciousness forever.

We explored Fairfield thoroughly in that first year, walking around the placid six-square-mile town. It felt like we were on an island of civilization—when you got to the edges of the city it was surrounded on all sides by endless rolling stretches of cornfields and pig farms.

After New York, Fairfield looked to me like an encyclopedia entry on small-town America. A white gazebo sat at the middle of the town square, and on summer nights, brass bands played there while senior citizens plopped down on lawn chairs to listen. When the music stopped the silence was powerful, broken only by the throbbing hum of the crickets. During the day, there was a constant drone of faraway tractors.

Around that square were dozens of small shops. There were drugstores with old glass jars in the windows and a photo studio filled with feathery-haired high school student photos. There was a steak house with a little door for kids to walk through and an Indian restaurant that inevitably made you sick to your stomach.

I didn't quite understand what I was seeing then, but Fairfield was a city that held two different and very opposing realities. There were the gurus and there were the townies and the way that they each thought life should be was very far apart.

In many ways, the arrival of Maharishi and all of his followers had been a godsend for Fairfield. Founded in 1839 and named for its natural beauty—rolling open fields for as far as the eye could see. The city sits in a remote and rural little pocket of southeast Iowa, not far from where Grant Wood painted his *American Gothic*.

Fairfield was the site of the first Iowa State Fair, and the first Carnegie library built outside Pennsylvania or Scotland—a gorgeous Gothic structure on the edge of the town square. Leading up to the Civil War, it was a stopping point for the Underground Railroad. The First Presbyterian Church in town dates back to 1841. There's also a Lutheran church, and a Methodist church. In the 1980s, an old glove factory was converted into a small synagogue for the growing group of Jewish meditators in Fairfield.

Parsons College was founded here in 1875 and for years enjoyed a solid reputation as a small Midwestern liberal arts school—until it became known as a party school and teetered into bankruptcy. Fairfield was both a college town and a factory town—after World War II, a number of manufacturers constructed brick factories on the outskirts of town to build washing machines and farming equipment.

Fairfield had been a thriving spot of American manufacturing but all of that was changing quickly and many of the factories were closed. When we walked past them, we would peek inside and imagine the alternate world that had once existed here.

As that first winter faded away into spring, we felt like we were in a wonderland. We spent long hours in the backyard, watching the ants gnaw open the peonies. There were mulberry trees everywhere, and the worn cement roads would be stained purple from their juice. We'd pack cups full of them and squish them into pulpy imaginary meals.

Stacey would run ahead along the gravel roads near our house on the edge of town, kicking at the dust, finding sticks to hit things with. I was always lagging behind everyone, daydreaming. Jeff teased me that I walked slowly on purpose—that I just wanted attention—but really I liked keeping myself a little apart from everyone else. I liked to get lost in my own head, imagining wild stories where I was the fearless protagonist, or just saying my mantra to myself. We finally felt like a family again, bound together in this strange new world.

Our first Thanksgiving dinner in Fairfield, we went over to Courtenay's house to eat. Stacey and I quietly filled our plates with the tofurkey and sweet potatoes and found a place to sit in the corner of the crowded living room. Mom had been whispering to her friends all afternoon. I knew something was going on; by the time we got back home that night and she sat us down on the couch for a talk, I was scared. Was she leaving? Would we have to move back to Florida with Grandma?

"I'm going to learn to fly," she said, her face crinkling up with excitement. She stared at us, waiting for us to share in her joy. She told us breathlessly that she was going to take a course to become a Siddha—an ancient Indian word that meant someone with superpowers, she explained—and learn to levitate and become Enlightened. She would now be one of a very small number of people in the world who knew how to fly. Hearing her say this made me think of Peter Pan telling Wendy that all you had to do was close your eyes and believe.

As we listened in our post-tofurkey haze, Mom told us how desperately she wanted to take the Taste of Utopia course—and help create World Peace—but it was only for meditators who knew how to fly, and learning cost thousands of dollars. I asked Mom why it cost so much money—after all, wasn't it just about believing? She explained that, according to the Maharishi, Americans didn't appreciate the value of things unless they paid for them. Then she excitedly added that someone had anonymously donated the money to pay for her tuition. This was Nature Support! She looked so happy telling us her big news, but I felt sadness rising inside. The Flying Course meant that she would have to spend two weeks on campus.

Who'll take care of us? I asked, my voice quivering.

"Are you going to leave us alone?" Stacey added sharply. Mom explained quickly, her words falling over each other, that two other kids whose parents were also taking the course were going to come stay at our apartment with us. Their babysitter would look after us. The way she said this, I knew there was no hope of changing her mind. Next to me on the couch, Stacey fiddled with the Mexican blanket that covered the threadbare cushions. He hated the kids who were coming to stay—we knew them from the neighborhood and they were wimpy and whiny and always smelled a little like boiled oats or old vegetables. Their mom always brought sour goat's milk for them to drink in their cereal when they came over to play.

Mom chattered on about how this was a once-in-a-lifetime opportunity, how the groups of people flying in Fairfield would change the world, how Maharishi had announced that we were at the dawn of a new era. She also talked about how now she would be able to spend time each day at the Golden Domes. When I went to bed that night, I stared out the window at the snowbanks for a long time and tried to imagine my mom soaring through the dark, crystalline sky. I knew I should want her to have superpowers, but really I just wanted her here at home with me.

CHAPTER FIVE

Taste of Utopia

I pushed out my breath and watched steam clouds form around my face. It was seven o'clock and it had been dark for hours—we were in the depths of our first full Iowa winter, almost a year after we'd moved to Fairfield. Around us, the campus streetlights cast a funny orange glow over the crowd, illuminating parkas, mittens, berets—all their colors bright against the gray of the surrounding snowbanks.

I stood close to my mother. In front of us and behind us, as far as I could see, a line of people snaked around The Shed, a metal building the size of a football field. I had never seen a building so long. In New York, the structures were narrow and shot up high in the air so that I had to crane my neck all the way back to see them touch the sky; this one extended horizontally, its low panels of shiny brown siding disappearing into the frozen darkness of the fields that sat just beyond Maharishi International University.

This was no ordinary shed. It had been built in a flurry of round-the-clock construction and all anyone seemed to talk about was when it would be finished, how many people it would hold, and what all those people gathered inside would mean for the future of the earth. It had been the center of conversation in our home for months.

This excitement was also shot through with anxiety—without The Shed, where would the seven thousand people who were expected for the Taste of Utopia gather?

Seven thousand. That number glowed golden in my head. Mom said it was an extraordinary number, Maharishi's number. Ancient Indian scriptures, correlated with modern science, according to Maharishi's researchers, said that if seven thousand people came together and meditated, they would create World Peace. This was called the Maharishi Effect.

Maharishi's researchers also found that when 1 percent of a community practiced TM, the crime rate was reduced by 16 percent. They even published a paper in which they calculated that "the coherence generated by group practice of the TM-Siddhi program should be proportional to the square of the number of participants." Because the world's population was then 4.9 billion, as my mom explained, it followed that we needed 7,000 people meditating to effect World Peace.

"Or something like that," she would conclude. She always gave this explanation quickly, and looking back now, I'm guessing that my mom—always a great math student and the daughter of an engineer—didn't want to look too closely at those numbers. Besides, she'd say, as if having a debate with herself, it feels so good—and so what else matters?

Over the past year, more and more followers had been arriving, and now the necessary seven thousand people had been added to Fairfield's base population, practically doubling it.

At that time, when I thought about World Peace, I pictured the whole planet becoming like a Care Bears cartoon: the sky would turn a bright blue, rainbows would float through the sky, delicious food would be everywhere for everyone, and life would be filled with glowing hearts and twinkling stars. We would have money to buy new coats every year and furniture and lots of toys for me. Stacey would stop hating me. We would become students of the Maharishi School. My dad would come back. My mom would be happy.

Outside The Shed, the line of people was boisterous, laughing in the darkness, their breath coming out in puffs of air that seemed to crystallize before vaporizing into the cold night. Above us, the stars felt especially close and bright. I was happily snuggled into my brand-new periwinkle coat. Periwinkle was my favorite color—my mom said it matched my eyes—and the coat was entirely mine, soft and blue, with fuzzy darker blue trim. It was an early Christmas present and I loved it. We were still broke but my mom had scraped together the money. I thought periwinkle sounded like something a fairy would wear. I loved the names of colors and when I came home in the afternoon after school, I would stretch out on the carpet of our house and open up the old cigar box with the picture of an Indian head on it that my mom had filled with her colored pencils from art school. We had every color of the rainbow and each one was a different length—depending on its popularity with me and Stacey—and I would beg Mom to tell me their names—lime, grass, azure, magenta, crimson, ochre, burnt umber . . . periwinkle.

The crowd shifted slowly forward through the snow as badges were being checked at the door. Mom had hung hers around her neck, over her coat. It said "Town Super Radiance" in big gold letters above a picture of Mom, her hair shiny, a funny half smile on her face. Underneath it said "Governor of the Age of Enlightenment: Siddha."

Siddha, Mom had told me, meant supernatural powers. It meant you could levitate.

Standing in line in the snow, I pulled on Mom's hand and asked her what it felt like to fly. She started laughing, in a way that kind of scared me, wild and loud. "It's the best thing in the world!" she said, continuing to laugh in loose gales.

I hadn't seen her in two weeks, not since she'd left for the Flying Course, and I just wanted to be near her. But out there with all those people she felt far away from me, part of something else, and I didn't understand what she was laughing about. The women standing next to us started laughing too as my mom explained to them what I had asked. "There are no words for it, honey," my mom said. "It's just like out of this world."

I blushed and decided to stop asking questions.

Maharishi's name was on the tip of everyone's tongue. Maharishi Mahesh Yogi, the greatest man alive. Our guru. Maharishi was coming. Maharishi was here! He would be here tonight—at last. What would he say? Would he be proud of us? Of The Shed? Of the seven thousand people? Of Fairfield, the town that, by the strength of his vision, had been transformed into a meditating peace engine?

At the entrance, a gray-haired lady scowled at us, her face framed by a big furry hat. Mom obediently pulled the laminated plastic badge from around her neck and the lady gave it a long stern glance, focusing her small pen flashlight on the photo of Mom, then looking up to examine her face. I felt an urgent knot of anxiety. What if we were turned away? But with a wave of her flashlight she sent us forward. Inside, The Shed felt like a huge aluminum castle, although it looked more like the site of an enormous indoor rodeo. Everyone's voices rippled off the metal, echoing through the vast space.

We stopped at the entrance area where all around us people were crouching to take off their snow- and mud-covered shoes. The sour-sweet smell of wet socks and shoes wafted through the air. Stacey and I pulled off our moon boots in a special spot we would remember. And then we followed Mom as she led the way past a golden rope and onto a sea of white-sheeted slabs of foam. I immediately started to bounce, springing up and down. People had staked out spots for themselves with their blankets and pillows and canvas folding seats, as if they were at an outdoor concert. We cut a path in between these encampments, looking for a place from which we would have a good view of Maharishi on stage.

I felt nervous, like anything could happen. What if Maharishi looked out across the crowd and could see inside me? What if he saw something bad? Would he know that I often got distracted during meditation? That I spent a lot of time thinking about things I wanted? That sometimes I couldn't empty my mind, that I wasn't always peaceful?

I also wondered if it would all happen that night the way the Maharishi had said it would. If all the wars would stop, if people would stop killing each other. I imagined the African kids I'd seen on TV, the skinny ones with potbellies covered in flies—I pictured a rain of food falling down on them from the sky.

We found a spot near some other parents who had established a kid-friendly zone and we dropped down among them. Mom put out two blankets she'd brought for us, and I sat next to Stacey, who was looking around for kids he knew. A big smile spread across his face as he took in the revelry. Everyone looked so happy! I looked ahead at the empty stage, awash in blinding lights.

Golden fabric was wrapped and draped all along the rim of the stage, and at the center stood an empty golden chair. It was surrounded by a wall of flowers—every kind of flower in the world it seemed, and in every color of the rainbow. It looked like a waterfall, cascading around this throne.

Finally, a man in a buttery yellow suit walked onto the stage and stood in front of the microphone. "Jai Guru Dev," he said into it, his voice slow and firm. He held a large conch shell. As the microphone gave off a static noise, the man raised the shell to his lips and blew. The huge crowd of people fell silent as the strange, tribal sound reverberated. People started to laugh—that same loose wild laughter my mom and her friends had had outside— and again, I didn't know why. Suddenly people were ringing bells. And then Mom was laughing too, and she too had a bell, a little brass bell that she withdrew from her pocket and rang along with everyone else. It didn't stop, the laughing and the conch shell and the bells. It felt like it went on forever. I felt something inside me lift up, my heart racing. And then suddenly there was only silence.

I could hear the rustle of pillows around me as the crowd watched a slow procession of kids file onto the stage. I heard low murmurs of parental pride ripple through the crowd. The kids onstage were the students of the Maharishi School of the Age of Enlightenment, their uniforms clean and crisp.

I wanted to be up there with them, dressed in a uniform, standing next to the throne, beaming with joy. They started to sing the Maharishi School anthem, their voices high and sweet.

Fortunate are we, to be born at a time such as this. Diving deep within The Self, we know that life is bliss! So we give thanks for the gift, of this knowledge heaven-sent!

Their bodies were stiff with pride as they belted out the name of the school—as if it were the greatest place on earth.

Young enlightened sages bringing peace to all on earth! So we give thanks, for the gift, of this knowledge Heaven sent and sing the praise, of Maharishi School of the Age of Enlightenmenttttttt.

Applause thundered through the vast hall, and people rang their little bells again. The students finished their song and left the stage, their pace deliberate and dignified, their faces shining with a sense of achievement.

Next, another man wearing a dark suit and a red tie walked onto the stage. He looked rich and important to me: his hair was dark and had an elegant side swoop and his face was boyish and round. This was Dr. Bevan Morris, the president of the university and Maharishi's right-hand man.

Bevan—or Dr. Morris as he was always introduced—was Australian but had been educated at Cambridge. To many, he exuded a snobby piety that had become the gold standard of decorum in the TM Movement. My mom said he had administered her teacher-training courses when she first learned how to be a TM instructor in Majorca, and that he had always been radically focused on furthering Maharishi's agenda. It was through him that much of Maharishi's Knowledge was disseminated to his followers throughout Fairfield.

"Maharishi spoke of this nation being on the doorstep of Utopia," he began, "of rising within itself into invincibility." His voice was trembling. "At this point, at this moment, on this day, we are no longer speaking of the doorstep of Utopia, we are speaking of the first Taste of Utopia for all mankind."

All around me the sound of bells was deafening, and I saw tears on the faces of many women nearby. My mom squeezed my knee and smiled at me, then closed her eyes to savor the moment.

"What we are speaking of here is not a movement of individual men or women or areas of the world or times or places. What we are speaking of here is a movement of the world itself. Not even nature itself could stop the shift of the world from complete ignorance to full Enlightenment at this time in history!"

Conch shells blew, bells tinkled again, and I felt perfectly located at this moment in time. This was it! A small figure draped in a white cloth emerged from the shadows on the side of the stage and shuffled slowly to the center. We were so far away from him that, to me, he looked like an ashen-faced child, but I could hear people gasping. My mom was staring at him, transfixed. She saw me looking at her and made a stern face at me and then closed her eyes. All around me, people were closing their eyes too. I looked down at my hands. My heart was beating so fast. I felt overwhelmed. Maharishi was here. The world was going to change. I closed my eyes and tried to repeat my mantra as I listened to the electric silence. I wanted to be a part of the wonder.

Over seven thousand people in this huge room, all focused on the space inside their heads. It felt infinite. My body shivered. I had never felt so good.

"We have such a beautiful gift for the world," Maharishi said slowly. "And only we know we have it! Only we can create Utopia. The Taste of Utopia seems to have been very sumptuous. We have proven to the world that this works. Here is a program that people do on their own," he said. He was silent for a moment. And then he burped. A big, froglike belch—as if he were at home alone rather than on a stage with thousands of people watching his every move. I peeked over to Stacey to see if he was laughing, but his eyes were closed.

Maharishi continued: "Here is the secret to a brilliant human race, because we are the custodians of this knowledge, we are the first generation in a long time to have discovered this secret functioning of natural law."

Everyone around me was locked into his words. Some people were slowly swaying from side to side as they sat in the lotus position.

"We are talking of a new civilization. No one will remain stressed, no one will remain hectic, everyone will fulfill one's wants," said the Maharishi with his lilting Indian accent. "If you want to achieve something, you work for it and you will achieve. Here we have the greatest expert at our command—the cosmic intelligence is at our command."

A few weeks later, when the crowds and their guru were gone, I heard Mom talking in a hushed voice on the phone to Courtenay about how the Fairfield sheriff's office had issued a subpoena for Maharishi to appear in court. Apparently, a disaffected follower had accused him of fraudulent practices, saying the mantra didn't work, that it didn't make you Enlightened. I thought of the dark fairy tale about the emperor with no clothes. But when I asked my mother about it, she brushed it off, saying it had been a silly misunderstanding and that she hoped it didn't mean Maharishi wouldn't return to what he liked to call "The Fair Field." We all knew his mantras worked—we had felt the power of transcending. And Enlightenment was dawning all around the world thanks to the practice of his meditation.

Around this time, we moved out of the crumbling little house that Boris had rented to us and into the upstairs half of a large old Victorian. We still had to tape plastic over the windows to keep the cold out, but it had two bedrooms and a big backyard. It was two doors away from school—which Stacey and I had since nicknamed "Stinkin' Lincoln"—and it looked like a real house. The kids from school assumed that we lived in the whole thing, not noticing the wooden porch that was cobbled onto the side of the house with our apartment door cut into it. The landlords had done a quick remodel when the crush of new people had begun to arrive for the Taste of Utopia. Still, I loved it. It felt like a tree house, and we could walk to school by ourselves.

I didn't understand what Jeff did for work but I did know that he had begun to travel a lot. Every time he returned from one of his business trips, he would bring me a little stuffed animal. Soon my bed was covered with these plush creatures—otters, foxes, bears, bunnies. At night I would curl up under the covers and surround myself with the little animals, burrowing myself into a warren with my feral family. I slept in the bottom bunk of a rickety wooden bed that someone had given my mom. Above me, Stacey creaked about, perpetually disgruntled and refusing to talk about what was happening around us. I nuzzled closer to my stuffed animals, whispering my love into their deaf ears.

Stacey made an exception for Jeff—they talked animatedly about the new video games that Jeff had tried on his sales trips. He'd also bring Stacey back cassette tapes of new music. I'd watch Stacey transform around him—become loose and silly in a way he hardly ever was with me anymore. Jeff started wearing nicer clothes—suits with red and navy ties, and leather loafers with little tassels on the top. He bought a sports car—a silver Honda Prelude with two seats in the front and a tiny backseat where Stacey and I could squeeze in. Jeff would drive us to the mall in Iowa City, where he would take Mom shopping. It felt like a dream come true watching her come out of the women's dressing room in a cotton-knit fuchsia sweater or heavy-shouldered blouses. She would giggle like a kid, and we would admire how beautiful she was. We'd stand around quietly when Jeff went to the register to pay, handing the cashier a shiny new credit card. I felt a funny feeling in my stomach knowing how broke we were. Mom would blush, quietly whispering that he didn't need to buy her anything, that it was too much.

In Fairfield, there was lots of talk about the prosperity that was coming thanks to the Maharishi Effect. Maharishi said we would all soon be living 200 percent of life—100 percent spiritual success and 100 percent material success. And I could tell that some people were really achieving that 200 percent because they had Nature's Support, and they were living in accordance with Maharishi's Natural Law—they were spiritually committed and it was paying off. Little offices seemed to be cropping up all over town with day-trading and other investment firms and software sellers, as well as tofu manufacturers and a big all-natural ice cream company. Mom and her friends talked about how much Nature was supporting us. And it was—the annual gross income for the county had nearly doubled in the last two years, and sales in the local stores had increased by 100 percent in the years since the Movement had arrived. Maharishi had said Fairfield was the Global Headquarters of World Peace, and this prosperity was seen as evidence of the dawning of Heaven on Earth right here in Iowa.

Fairfield felt like a boomtown, like we were on the frontier in the midst of a gold rush. When Maharishi had asked people to come to Fairfield, he'd promised them "wealth and wisdom squared." And, for some, it came true. Since the meditators had descended on Fairfield, four hundred new businesses had opened. With their three-hour program as the cornerstone of their daily lives, entrepreneurs could go from the dome and harness Nature Support and then go out and make money. Some were small—a falafel shop, a tofu manufacturer, but there were suddenly thriving new businesses in town. A series of new office towers were built near the railroad tracks, with two-story lobbies and plant-filled atriums.

My brother's friend Ben, a skinny doe-eyed kid, lived on the other side of town in a large, somewhat ramshackle mansion. Ben's dad was Ed Beckley, now often referred to as the father of American infomercials. Ed started the Beckley Group in the early '80s and then, like us, was drawn to be a part of his guru's movement in Fairfield. In 1985 the Fairfield-based Beckley Group was doing hundreds of millions of dollars in sales by selling Beckley's "Millionaire-Maker," program, a $299 kit of cassettes that promised to teach people how to get rich quick in real estate. He even had a money-back guarantee. In 1985, he estimated his own net worth at $25 million. Ed Beckley gave his two-day, $595 seminar to hundreds of thousands of people around the country (including current motivational superstar Tony Robbins, who praised Beckley as an early inspiration). Ed was held up as an inspiration in town—an example of Maharishi's Knowledge in action. And he wasn't the only one.

The San Francisco–based commodities brokerage International Trading Group Ltd. opened a Fairfield office in the early '80s after several California brokers had wanted to heed Maharishi's call. Soon the office was posting the highest sales figures of all of ITG's eight branch offices. Salesmen were making upward of $20,000 a month and suddenly they were driving their golden luxury vehicles around town and buying their wives fur coats. Meditators established their own Sidha Golf Association and the Sidha Travel Service. There was the Heaven on Earth novelty shop and real estate agency. Instead of aligning themselves with the local chamber of commerce, meditators started their own Chamber of Prosperity and Progress.

This whirlwind of success felt like proof that our decision to move here was correct. With Jeff, we felt like we were also part of this rising prosperity. He bought a little Victorian house on the other side of town. It was pale brown with chocolate-colored trim, and it had three bedrooms. When he took us over to show us around, Stacey and I quickly darted from room to room, trying to decide which one we would take. But Mom and Jeff didn't say anything about us moving in, so we didn't ask. We just waited.

Meditation for me at the time was a subtle alternate reality to which I liked to escape. By saying my mantra to myself, I could pop out of whatever situation I was in, or whatever feelings I was having, and be in a familiar quiet place, my head empty of thoughts. Around me that quiet familiarity was being celebrated as the Unified Field, the source of all creation that we were all sharing with the world through our practice of meditation. There was a sense of energy and excitement about it—as if we had all discovered some sort of Fountain of Life. I couldn't really connect the big cosmic excitement about meditation to my own silent practice. I liked the idea of it all, but for me my mantra was like a small secret door that would take me away from the world around me.

A few months after the Taste of Utopia course ended, just as the snow was melting, Mom came home with great news. As with her flying course, a mysterious donor (later to be revealed as yet another male admirer of hers) had offered to pay for Stacey and me to go to the Maharishi School. We were thrilled! Mom seemed embarrassed and somehow a little angry when she delivered the news to Jeff that someone else was paying for us. But Jeff didn't seem to notice, giving us big hugs and hearty congratulations, although his eyes felt like they were looking elsewhere, far away.

CHAPTER SIX

Fortunate Are We!

As I shuffled into the Maharishi School that first February morning, sunlight streamed in through the big bright windows. Large charts hung on the walls. In a big, friendly gold font, they spelled out the basics of our guru's knowledge: Maharishi's Sixteen Principles of SCI. SCI, I quickly learned, stood for the Science of Creative Intelligence: it was Maharishi's philosophy of everything. There was a picture of him on every wall and gold scroll-like posters quoting his wisdom about the fundamental truths of the world. His principles were written everywhere you looked:

1. Nature of life is to grow
2. Order is present everywhere
3. Life is found in layers
4. Outer depends on Inner
5. Seek the highest first
6. Rest and activity
7. Enjoy greater efficiency and accomplish more
8. Every action has a reaction
9. Purification leads to progress
10. The field of all possibilities is the source of all solutions

11. Thought leads to action, action leads to achievement, and achievement leads to fulfillment
12. Knowledge is gained from inside and outside
13. Knowledge is structured in consciousness
14. Harmony exists in diversity
15. Wholeness is contained in every part
16. Whole is greater than sum of the parts

For me, those principles seemed a serene mastery over the chaos of the world and I immediately committed them to heart. On that first day of school, the teacher introduced me to the twenty second-graders who were sitting with their hands folded on their desks, and each one beamed at me. Kids came up and offered to share, asked me questions about where I had come from and what things I liked to do. I'd never met kids like this.

Unlike public school, I wasn't the only new kid in the class, or the only one whose family wasn't from Iowa. There were kids from India, Europe, California—everywhere. No one was actually from Iowa!

To me, the school felt like home. It reminded me of New York where everyone was so different from everyone else. On the first day, I told Mrs. Tachet a lie: I said that I had just moved here to Iowa from New York City. I looked around, wondering if any of the girls staring at me knew that I had been living four blocks away for the last year and a half, going to the townie school. But no one appeared to know my secret, and soon they were teasing me for having a New York accent. Everyone called me the Red Apple, because I was from the Big Apple and I blushed so much. I played it up—drawing out my *o*'s just a little bit longer. I wanted to be from anywhere besides Stinkin' Lincoln.

At public school, class had started at 7:50 a.m. The shrill alarm of the school-wide bell signaled the start of school. Beneath the blaze of fluorescent lights, I would sit at my desk while my teachers did the roll call, army-sergeant style.

Maharishi said that the Nature of Life was Bliss and that Right Action was always to be Effortless. Given that, the school day began around 9:30 in the morning with free play. Each morning Stacey and I had to walk past our old school in order to get to the Maharishi School. In my crisp navy uniform and red bow tie, I felt like a slow-moving target. If my old classmates were outside when we passed, they'd all stand at the fence, rattling the chain and screaming, "Guru!" at the top of their lungs.

Arrival felt casual—Mom would drop us off at the three-story redbrick building after she'd returned from her two-hour meditation at the dome. The Maharishi School was nestled in the valley of a small hill at the southern tip of the campus. It looked to me like something out of a storybook—with ivy crawling up the edges of the school and white columns. Inside, the hallways were covered in artwork and banners of Maharishi's sayings.

Once we had all gathered in the classroom, our teacher would quiet us down and then ring a small brass bell. "Jai Guru Dev," she would whisper. This phrase was said constantly at school, and of course I'd known that it meant "Praises to Guru Dev" since I'd been given my Word of Wisdom. Now our teachers said it to begin and end our meditation, always in a gentle voice, as if the expression itself were a slide into some other heightened state of consciousness.

And it wasn't just for meditation—people would use it as a greeting and as a good-bye—it was almost a way of reminding us all that we were blessed to be here in this moment right now. Once we finished our meditation, we would always start the day with SCI class. We did this, our teacher explained, so that throughout the day Maharishi's knowledge would illuminate everything we learned.

Sitting at our desks, we hurried to carefully fold our hands and show that we were ready. We would face the teacher and sing the song that began each day:

It's time for SCI. It's time for SCI. The Science of Creative Intelligence, the Knowledge of the fullness of life. It's the practical application of Transcendental Meditation.

We would then dive into Maharishi's Knowledge, reciting his principles in order, or focusing on a specific one, like Water the Root to Enjoy the Fruit, and would illustrate it quietly at our desks. We drew crude brown oak trees and thunderous blue rain clouds. If pushed, I could easily explain how the roots of the tree reaching underneath the ground were an example of the fundamental process of nature going to the deepest source, Maharishi's Unified Field, and that from there the roots would tap the unbounded source of all creation and carry that vitality up through the tree trunk to the branches, blossoming into leaves and flowers, a manifestation of the infinite creativity and possibility of all things.

Here at the Maharishi School, I quickly learned that what we wanted to do was experience the world the way that Maharishi did. That seemed to be why everyone started every sentence with "Maharishi says . . ." Doing so seemed to shift your perspective a little, helping you imagine what things might look like if you were a superpowered Enlightened person instead of just regular old you.

Though I was only seven years old, I felt part of the humming bigness that was the Transcendental Meditation Movement at that time. It was a beehive of activity, filled with men and women rushing to and fro along the crumbling walkways. Dressed in long skirts and suits, they were organizing retreats, printing brochures and books of Maharishi's knowledge, designing classes and new curriculums and workshops to disseminate ideas that were going to change the world. This campus was the Global Headquarters for Heaven on Earth and it felt like it.

During the week, we would get to explore the campus—many of our classes were held inside the facilities of the Maharishi International University. On our way to our PE and drama classes, we would walk past neuroscientists in lab coats who were spending their days measuring the effects of TM on the brain. Even for lunch, we would join our families and the larger university—professors, students, and staff—to eat at the campus cafeteria. We'd march past the grand sign announcing the dining hall's name: "ANNA-PURNA." Inside the light was dim, the ceiling low. As we entered, I could glimpse a room that was mostly screened off from the rest. A little sign read "SILENT DINING, Jai Guru Dev." I could see people inside, sitting at a table, facing straight forward, not speaking to one another; they faced the wall, their faces blank as they focused entirely on their chewing. There were rumors that Maharishi had advised that the ideal amount of chews per bite was thirty-two.

I would line up alongside my classmates, take a tray, and make my way down the line. The meals varied very little—there was always rice, dal, and a mush of steamed vegetables. And then some sort of variation on tofu—barbecued, curried, breaded, steamed, sautéed, scrambled, grilled. Maharishi encouraged a vegetarian diet—he ate rice and dal, so we ate rice and dal.

If I was sitting with my class, we'd gather at a table and our teacher would ring a bronze bell that she carried with her. First we said the Vedic prayer that Maharishi had asked us all to say before meals. We'd say it once in Sanskrit, mumbling the words, and then quietly again in the English translation given us:

Saha nav avatu
Saha nau bhunaktu
Saha viryam karavavahai
Tejaswi nav adhitam astu
Ma vidwishavahai

Let us be together,
Let us eat together,
Let us be vital together,
Let us be radiating truth, radiating the light of life.
Never shall we denounce anyone, never entertain negativity.

We shouted, "Jai Guru Dev!" at the end, in unison, often feeling more hungry than thankful. We dug into the food, trying to remember to count each bite as we chewed. We'd return to the classroom for some spelling, a little math, and more SCI. School finished around four o'clock, ending with another five-minute meditation. With that last Jai Guru Dev, to close our Word of Wisdom, we waited for our parents to come pick us up before they went to the dome. Throughout the day, I felt a quiet self-awareness that I hadn't experienced at Stinkin' Lincoln. With consciousness a constant topic of classroom discussion, my mind felt like it kept turning around to look at itself. My own growing awareness of that quietness in itself felt like evidence that supported Maharishi's idea of the world as unified and silent.

*   *   *

After a few months, I could barely remember what life had been like before the Maharishi School. Everything felt so easy there. Everyone wanted to be experiencing and emanating bliss and that meant that our teachers indulged us in ways I could never have imagined. If I got sleepy during class, it was perfectly acceptable to put my head down on the desk and get some rest. After all, according to Maharishi, Rest and Activity were the Basis of Life.

I had, by then, learned the particular language of the Movement. There were words and phrases that were used constantly by my teachers and administrators that I came to realize were like philosophical polestars for us.

The most important of these was "Being on the Program." Being on the Program was what living in Fairfield was all about. It meant that you were following Maharishi's directions to become Enlightened. It meant that you went to the dome every day, twice a day, to meditate and fly. Over time it came to mean more—that the way you ate, slept, built your home, wore your jewels, and looked to the stars were in accord with Maharishi's vision.

The whole point of Being on the Program was to achieve Maharishi's level of consciousness (there were seven layers of consciousness, according to Maharishi, ranging from waking to sleeping to Cosmic and Unity consciousness). I understood that Maharishi had the highest level of consciousness of anyone and if we kept practicing TM, we could climb a ladderlike series of levels until we got to be like him—blissful.

Bliss was basically another name for Enlightenment, but it was in a more conversational way that my mom and her friends and our teachers liked to talk about it. Less intimidating sounding than Enlightenment, I guess. Still, bliss was big. Bliss meant you were meditating right and that you were accessing the Unified Field and experiencing reality accurately. You could also experience it briefly, like sometimes I heard teachers use it to describe a really fun time, such as: How was your trip to Maui? Oh, it was so blissful, it was twenty-four-hour bliss!

Of course, bliss wasn't only casual. Sometimes it was an intense experience. This was probably why Maharishi seemed sort of spaced out during some of the many videotapes that we watched of him during school assemblies. He would stare into the distance, caressing the flower in his lap, and then he'd just start laughing. And you could hear the audience on the video laugh too, which of course made our teachers laugh, like life was actually this big beautiful joke, if only you took the time to look at it. The way Maharishi did.

There was a name for that spontaneous laughter: Bubbling Bliss. While people often got it listening to Maharishi, it was usually something adults said happened when they were flying. But it could happen at the dinner table, over barbecued tofu and veggies, when people would erupt in sudden cascades of laughter that everyone knew was Bubbling Bliss.

The opposite of Bubbling Bliss though was Entertaining Negativity. This was the worst! We were cautioned all the time not to do it—even though it seemed like it often happened outside our control. Entertaining Negativity could be worrying about something bad or scary happening or it could be applied simply when you were being mean to someone else. Because we all knew well Maharishi's saying, "What You Put Your Attention On Grows in Your Awareness!" We knew our thoughts had the power to shape things and it was important to focus them on positive things all the time.

After my first quarter, my teacher looked at me and saw the reflected glory of Maharishi's Knowledge glowing back at her: "Claire can soften any heart. I really enjoy having her in my class—her presence enlivens Being," she wrote on my first report card. I had received an A in SCI, showing that I could relate Maharishi's principles to my own behavior. And also that I had a "smooth practice of TM."

As a new student at the Maharishi School, I felt like I'd entered a beautiful bubble. From morning to night, I was surrounded by Maharishi's vision and people who were entirely focused on carrying it out. Everything was so hopeful, our potential was so abundant, the mission was so powerful. Sometimes though, it exhausted me.

In the spring after I started school, I woke up one morning and my head felt thick and my vision blurred. I had a fever, again. For as long as I remembered I'd been prone to getting sick. I was born with a small esophagus, and when I was two years old, a botched operation to stretch it ended up puncturing my lungs. I ended up with a massive scar along my right side, a sort of Frankenstein-style mark that for years I tried to hide. My mother had tended to me during that time like a dutiful nurse, putting all my food in a blender until I was four. Even after that emergency had passed, she doted on me when I was sick—ear infections, fevers, asthma, or the flu. Though I was sick a lot, going to the doctor was a last resort. Mostly Mom consulted a home health book that she had from the seventies, mixing up herbs and teas and insisting we lie down and rest together.

That morning I climbed into my mom's bed as she was finishing her meditation. When she greeted me with a hello a few minutes later—the sign that she was finished—I told her I was sick. She felt my forehead and my stomach, and murmured agreement that I was hot.

"You'll need to take some herbs," she said, looking a little distracted. She couldn't miss work. Now eight, I wasn't quite old enough to stay home alone. I reassured her I would be fine, that I'd lock the door.

The sunlight was muted coming in. My mother and Stacey tromped out the door in boots and hats and coats. And then it was quiet. I loved this time when I could be totally alone in our house, without any restriction. But when I went to bed, I didn't wake up until I heard my mom's key in the lock. She had come home to make me lunch.

She took her coat off and hung it in the crowded hallway rack and peeled off her boots. She wore a long flowered skirt, dark hose, and a bright sweater. Her eyes sparkled from little stripes of blue eyeliner. She looked beautiful. She felt my forehead. When she heard I'd slept the whole time, she looked happy. I slumped in the chair and watched her as she went about cooking. She diced onions and peppers, combining them with chunks of tofu. The smell of turmeric and oil filled the air.

She listened attentively as I told her about the book I was reading, *The Last Unicorn*. She laughed as I described in rigorous detail the fantastical world. When I finished, she looked at me. "You really get lost in these books, don't you? You are so smart, honey, it's amazing."

I loved being alone with my mom; she rarely had time to pay attention to me like this. When we were alone together she was more gentle and thoughtful with me than when she was herding Stacey and me around or rushing to work or The Program. She turned away from me to start mixing up some herbal mixture she'd concocted. "I'm designing this little rabbit at work that you would love," she said. "He's so fat and short!" Mom had taken a job designing stuffed animals and she would regale me with stories of her creations. She handed me a little saucer of honey and something dark and earthy smelling. I whined about the taste and she ignored me. I choked it down with a glass of water and she petted my hair.

"You know you're the most important thing in the world to me, right?" she said, her blue eyes wet with emotion. I nodded. "I wish I could stay home and take care of you." I nodded again. I wished that too. Then she put on her coat and went back to work.

I couldn't stop thinking about another book I'd just finished, *The Girl with the Silver Eyes.* I'd checked it out from the library—something about the plain-faced blond girl on the cover staring hypnotically out at me had drawn me toward it. I'd picked out the book on Friday, and I had already read it twice over the weekend. It was the story of a girl named Katie whose parents were divorced and who was an outsider because she was smarter than everyone else and had special powers. I couldn't turn the pages fast enough because I identified with her so completely. The way she seemed to be always watching people and thinking about what they did instead of joining in. The way some kids avoided her or adults didn't seem to understand her. I liked that it was because she was so smart, not because she was weird. Well, she was a little weird. She had a special power called telekinesis. She could move things with her mind.

For example, if her mom told her to clean up her room, she could simply concentrate really hard and snap, her room would be in perfect order. This was my fantasy. And, given that my mom could fly, it did not seem unattainable.

I spent a lot of time thinking about powers—Mom said that the Flying Course had changed her. Whenever I asked about it she would get a faraway look and say, "It just feels so good, honey. It's out of this world!" The idea that Mom was flying and feeling this way was so intriguing to me. The more I meditated, the more I thought I would have special abilities too. I sensed the world was filled with hidden powers—abilities that Maharishi could give us. You just needed to know the right mantras to access them. My mom's friends in Fairfield always remarked on how lucky we were to learn meditation so young. "Imagine," they'd say, "you'll probably be Enlightened by the time you are a teenager." Even our teachers treated us like chosen ones—Maharishi had said we at my school were Brahmin reincarnated, fortunate to be born when we were and selected because of an infinite lifetime of good karma to be the leaders of the Age of Enlightenment.

So after reading *The Girl with the Silver Eyes*, I took on a new challenge. During our silent Word of Wisdom meditation in the mornings at school, I'd sit at my desk and try to get objects—a piece of paper, a pencil, a crayon—to move telekinetically. So far I hadn't had any luck.

One day, after the teacher pronounced the ending of our Word of Wisdom with her ceremonial whisper of "Jai Guru Dev," she pointed to one of the posters on the wall that was made to look like a scroll. "Every Action Has a Reaction." Mrs. Stevenson asked if anyone could tell her an example of actions having a reaction and all around me, hands wiggled in the air.

I turned my attention to my pencil. Brand new, yellow, with bright green writing along the side spelling out "TICONDERO-GA." And a pink eraser, untouched. I concentrated as hard as I could, using my third eye.

Next to me, a boy named Evrim whose parents had moved here from Turkey was explaining that if you eat something, later on you will poop, and how this was a reaction to an action. Kids began to laugh wildly. I looked up and snorted a little to myself. The teacher gave him a stern look. I stared back down at my desk. "I can do this," I thought. "I am special. I have superpowers just like my mom, just like Maharishi, just like Luke Skywalker."

I glanced at the large framed photograph of Maharishi hanging next to a smaller head shot of President Ronald Reagan. Maybe Maharishi was watching me right now, maybe he sensed that I had this gift?

I silenced the thoughts in my head. I imagined the Unified Field and I summoned its powers, feeling energy coursing through my body. My eyes burned as very slowly I watched the pencil begin to roll from one side of the desk to the other. For a brief moment, the world stopped and it was just that pencil and me, connected to some larger power. My heart started beating so fast. My shoulders seized up. I felt like I'd been slapped out of a dream. I put my hand over the pencil and looked up, thinking that the entire room was staring at me. But no one was paying any attention. My cheeks flushed. I felt like Maharishi had reached out of his photograph on the wall and chosen me. Did I have special powers now? Like Maharishi?

I was never able to move anything with my mind again and sometimes I wonder now if I imagined the whole thing. Or if for a moment I had gained the mind control that everyone around me was striving for. Either way, it was a clear sign of my own growing sense of the power endowed by the TM Movement. I believed in our potential to do phenomenal things, as Maharishi did. I believed that I would one day levitate all on my own. I believed that by connecting to the Unified Field I would bring about World Peace and the Dawn of the Age of Enlightenment.

*   *   *

Not long after the day I moved the pencil, at the grocery store with my mom at the checkout, I saw a bright yellow-and-red glossy poster with starbursts amid the tattered handmade signs offering gem-stone consultations and discounted herbal supplements.

"CIRCUS," it read. I drew closer, breathless. Juggling, fire breathing, tightrope walking. "Mom!" I shouted. There was an actual circus here in Iowa?

Then I saw the picture—an illustration of a majestic white unicorn at the bottom of the poster. "The Living Unicorn," it read.

I had read *The Last Unicorn* at least three times. I drew unicorns endlessly in my school notebooks. I read the small print underneath the cameo portrait. "Believe with all your heart that impossible dreams can happen. Close your eyes and count to three . . . you'll see your wish come true!"

"Moooom," I moaned, grabbing her sleeve as she heaved a grocery bag onto her shoulder. "Mom, Mom, the circus is coming to Fairfield. AND THERE'S A UNICORN!"

Mom's mouth crinkled up into a funny smile. "I'm not sure, honey, do you really want to do something like that? It looks kind of . . . sleazy." Yes, I assured her, I did want to do it. I had to do it. I was going to do it. She rolled her eyes. "Well, let's see what I can do."

In the days and weeks that followed, I became obsessed with seeing "The Living Unicorn." As we sat down to our rice and dal dinner, I'd launch into a speech about the wonder and magic of unicorns. I wondered where it had come from and whether it liked living in the circus and traveling to places like Fairfield, Iowa. I wondered if it would have sparkles shimmering the way unicorns did in the cartoons, or if it would just look like a regular horse with a really pretty horn. Privately, I wondered if it would recognize me as its superpowered partner and we might run off together to an enchanted kingdom.

One late-summer afternoon, Mom and Jeff drove me out to the fairgrounds, but the circus wasn't open yet. It was getting close to five o'clock—Program Time—so they were both in a hurry to go to the dome and fly. Jeff asked the guy selling tickets about "The Living Unicorn." "Would it be possible for me to just peek?" he asked, his hands on my shoulders, stepping me forward toward the gatekeeper just a bit. The man, wearing a striped vest and a bow tie, mumbled something about his bosses, looked around furtively, and then quickly led me over to a small striped tent.

My heart was pounding. The man lifted the flap and I stepped inside, alone. In my memory—one of my clearest from that age—a single beam of dusty sunlight came through the top of the tent and illuminated the animal at the center. I blinked. I stared. And then I tried immediately to un-see what was before me. A meek white goat was chained to a rusty peg, which had been pounded into the center of the dirt floor. On the top of its head sat a single swollen-looking horn. Around it, the skin looked red and irritated—as if the horn had been somehow surgically attached or sewn on. Both were too terrible to imagine. I felt dizzy as I walked up and gave the animal a gentle pat, and it looked up at me with milky, sad eyes. I turned around and walked out.

I didn't want to look at my mom or Jeff—I felt like all the adults around me had conspired to deceive me. The shoddiness of what I'd seen stung given all that I had so happily imagined. How could they trick people this way? I thought. Couldn't everyone see that it wasn't real?

CHAPTER SEVEN

Utopia Park

More and more, Jeff was traveling for work, and when he returned he was exhausted and distracted. Mom laughed less and seemed to me quiet and distant when he was there. She got a perm—transforming her silky, straight hair into a loose Afro of curls. Sensing instability, both Stacey and I clung to him, pushing each other out of the way to get near him.

When he came over for dinner after Program Time, it didn't feel quite as cozy as it had. There'd be a weird hush at the table. Soon after, they would shut themselves in my mother's room across the hall. Later, I'd hear the front door shut softly and I'd find Mom in the kitchen wet faced and red eyed. We had figured they would get married—their friends were always asking when it was going to happen. But now Jeff wasn't acting like that was the plan: the tiny new two-seat sports car, the house he had renovated with a fragile glass coffee table and track lighting. Looking back, I realized these were the signs of a life that didn't include us after all.

Mom had spent the last few years working with a lawyer to try to divorce my dad. He had no permanent address and wouldn't respond to the letters she sent in care of his friends and family. She'd gone so far as to post notices in newspapers asking my father to appear in court, but even that hadn't worked. In April of that year, Maharishi had asked for Siddhas to meditate longer in the dome, in a heightened effort at World Peace he called "Miracle Month." For Mom, it felt like it had been her own personal Miracle Month. Shortly thereafter, however, she got word that the divorce had at last gone through without my dad's consent. She felt an enormous sense of relief that that chapter of her life was over. Maybe she could start something new.

But it was also during Miracle Month that Jeff broke off with her. He told her she should find a good guy to settle down with. He said he couldn't ignore the siren call of Enlightenment. He wanted to focus on his spiritual pursuits, so he was going to rejoin Purusha, the monkish order of celibate men who meditated all the time and served Maharishi's wishes. This is what he'd been doing when we arrived in Fairfield.

To me, meditating all the time seemed as silly a thing to do as drinking all the time. What was so uncomfortable about being a grown-up that you had to drink or meditate your way through it? I was crushed. From the few movies I'd been allowed to see, I knew that some people had families and relationships that lasted for years, that people stayed together and loved each other and just went about their lives—driving in station wagons and sitting on porches talking. I didn't understand why my parents and Jeff couldn't just be comfortable with how things were.

Overnight, Jeff disappeared from our lives and Mom said we needed to find a new place to live. She said she couldn't live somewhere with plastic on the windows and no thermostat. She went on a mission. When she told us she had managed to secure a three-bedroom trailer in Utopia Park, I felt like I'd won the lottery.

At last we could leave our apartment on the townie side of Fairfield and move onto campus. We would live by the Golden Domes and be a part of everything taking place at the Maharishi International University. There we could live in the brand-new two-hundred-home trailer park just for meditators! Stacey let out a cheer and we exchanged glances. This meant we could have our own bedrooms. I could put up my posters of horses and Stacey could transfer his collage of ripped-out pages from skate magazines from our bunk bed to the walls of his own room.

But the most important thing was that we would be far away from the jeering kids at Stinkin' Lincoln and cocooned in the safety of an all-meditator community. We wouldn't have to make the humiliating journey every morning past our old schoolmates playing in the yard at morning recess, rattling the chain-link fence and shouting, "Guru! Guru!"

Our new address was Utopia Park, 1K, a brand-new trailer made of contrasting shades of brown aluminum. Along one side, a row of baby poplar plants lined a gravel path. On the other side was a small plot of grass where Mom said we could plant flowers and vegetables. On all sides, from every window, we had a perfect view of the other 199 trailers.

By the end of moving day, the boxes were stacked so high inside our new home that they touched the ceiling. Mom cheerfully said good-bye to the friends who had helped us move and closed the synthetic wood door behind them. It made a hollow sound. She turned and made her way over to the polyester brown basket-weave couch—part of a set of itchy synthetic furniture that had come with the place.

"We won't stay here long," she said to us, looking overwhelmed by how quickly we'd filled up the space. "We're going to get a real house soon. The jyotishi said that I'm entering a new astrological period of great abundance." She blew her nose and excused herself to go meditate.

I wandered off to my own room. I could do whatever I wanted now, without having to worry about annoying Stacey. I sat cross-legged on the floor, surrounded by my boxes and imagined what life would be like in here. It felt strange and wonderful to be away from Mom and Stacey in a space that was just my own.

I heard Mom yell from the other end of the trailer that it was time to do my Word of Wisdom, so I climbed on the bed, shut my eyes, and started to say my mantra to myself, but I could barely focus on the simple sound. My mind was quickly filling up with what living in Utopia Park would mean. It meant new friends. It meant walking to school through the wooded path that led across campus. It meant we could walk to the domes for all the big celebrations—satellite phone calls from Maharishi and holidays like Guru Purnima and Maharishi's birthday. We were safe inside the dream world that was Maharishi's campus.

At the Maharishi School, living at Utopia Park was considered enviable—there were so many kids living there that it felt like camp. When Mom went to The Program, we had total freedom. It was as if the campus itself had become our babysitter, and it was a very permissive one. On a spring afternoon, Stacey was in the kitchen concocting some kind of carrot and mustard snack when Mom came through the door in a huff. She immediately yelled at him to go bring the groceries in from the car, and he kicked my ankle as he walked outside.

I felt a wave of guilt as she made her way through the house and past me, buried in the couch, reading one of my Sweet Valley High books. She barked orders for me to get up and help her put the groceries away. I instantly felt lazy, spoiled. She saw the dishes in the sink and her mood went from bad to worse. Stacey and I hurried to put things away, to try to soothe her nerves and prove that we weren't so awful. She came back from her bedroom in her soft dome clothes, keeping her eyes away from us, and moved quickly through her stretches and breathing exercises, inhaling strongly through her nose.

I wandered off to my room, politely agreeing to the chores she asked me to do while she was at the dome. I heard the metal door of the trailer slam and her footsteps on the gravel path outside. For a moment there was true silence as I sat in my room, pretending to meditate—as promised. I heard the spring poplars outside, brushing against the metal of the trailer. I said my mantra and I felt a weight lifting. She was gone, along with the anxiety and the guilt that I felt because I should have been doing something else.

After a few minutes of meditating—shaving a little time off my mandated eight minutes—I went out in the living room and found Stacey, who immediately leaped to his feet from the couch where he'd been doing his own halfhearted mantra. He opened the door and yelled across the street to another kid, and I followed him outside.

The road was quiet but for the sound of metal doors clanging. The space between the trailers was thick with new grass and the smell of daffodils wafted through the air. Kids started coming up the block, congregating near the intersection of our house. They were mostly older than me, but I was included because of Stacey. I plopped down on a railroad beam, and watched as the group argued about what game we would play. Above us the sky was a robin's egg blue, with the orange of the sunset nibbling at the margins. Stacey shouted to me that we were playing Ghost in the Graveyard and he would be the zombie. He started to count, his cheeks flushed and excited as he bossed the rest of us around. I ran off, ducking and weaving between the trailers.

Afterward, sitting in a clearing between trailers, we all lay down, exhausted. David, a kid my brother's age, suggested we go over to the frats, across the street from Utopia Park, and see if we could steal money from the soda machines. The frats were crumbly yellow brick buildings that had been the fraternity houses for Parsons but now staff for the university occupied them. We raced over as a herd, shouting Comanche war cries and made our way into the basement of one of the frats. I inhaled the smell of old socks and Indian spices. I felt scared—what if someone saw us here? Would Mom get kicked out of the dome? There was an old Pepsi machine in the corner of the threadbare lobby—covered in a thin layer of dust. Soda wasn't really part of pursuing Enlightenment. The older kids took turns kicking the machine, pounding on it in strategic spots. Inside, the cans of soda rattled, until finally, like a slot machine, coins poured out of the change hole. We shrieked, all of us grabbing at the nickels and dimes until we heard the sound of a door upstairs slam.

"Jai Guru Dev?" said a man's voice sternly, like a question.

It was James, the head of campus security. We all lived in fear of James—he was a squat black guy from Chicago who had supposedly once been a cop. This was often cited as a reason for his taking the patrolling of our Utopian campus so seriously. This was intended to keep away ne'er-do-well townie kids who liked to come through and vandalize 'ru cars. But James seemed to spend most of his time scaring the crap out of us meditator kids instead. Without a word, we all raced out the basement door, coins jingling in our pockets. As the sky started to darken, we separated from the others, and hurried back to 1K. I felt guilty but euphoric.

Life was a little lonelier now with Jeff gone. A quietness had settled over the house. Though my mom had a sly, quirky sense of humor, she wasn't particularly outgoing. She was incredibly sensitive, and in our house, we were always careful with the way we spoke to each other. Stacey and I followed her lead—we were an introverted family. Jeff had opened us up to the community, engaging people in line at the store, acquaintances we saw at dome celebrations. With him gone, it felt like we drew back into the small shell of our family.

Mom seemed intent though on making sure Stacey had "positive male role models." I guess that was the thinking when she introduced Lon Ritzo into our lives, a short fat guy she'd met at work. At her latest job, she designed small stained glass ornaments for gift catalogs. After school, I would walk to her office on the third floor of an old brick industrial building alongside the railroad tracks. She sat at her large drafting desk and I would climb under it, setting myself up with books and stuffed animals while she finished her last hour before Program Time. I'd conjure up little skits with the animals as my mom drew hibiscus and hummingbirds on the desk above. Lon slowly befriended me, and then my brother. He would stand in the doorway of the reception area and joke with us as we sat waiting for Mom to take us home. Sometimes he'd offer to take us down the hall for a soda or a snack from the vending machine and Mom would seem relieved to have us out of her hair.

After a while, Mom started dropping us off at Lon's apartment after work, before she went to the dome. Stacey had a friend who lived in the same apartment building, and there were tons of meditator kids who would hang around Lon's apartment. Somehow, every kid seemed to be his friend. But I understood we were special, we were his favorites. As the youngest, I'd often stay behind with Lon and watch TV and eat snacks like vanilla wafers and orange soda—all of the junky, artificially flavored food that he seemed to keep just for me—nudging me slyly and making me promise not to tell Mom.

One afternoon, while Mom was at the dome, we were alone in his dim apartment, sunlight streaming in through half-shut blinds. Stacey wasn't there. I said I wanted to watch TV and Lon said, no, let's do something different. "Aren't you bored with TV?" he asked. I looked at him, his pudgy face streaked on the edges with lines of sweat. I wasn't bored with TV—it was forbidden and I wanted to watch it whenever I could.

Lon asked me, if I could do anything to him what would I do? I felt the challenge of it—I was supposed to think of something really wild, something that wasn't allowed. He smiled a funny sort of half smile at me. I looked around the bare apartment and back at his lumpy fat body. "I want to pour lime ice cream onto your chest from the top of your refrigerator," I said.

Lon laughed but a sort of disappointment flickered across his face at the same time. He hoisted me up onto the countertop, his hands around my narrow hips, and from there I climbed up on top of his dusty refrigerator. Hidden up there like some sort of wild animal from a storybook, I laughed as I looked down at him—he looked so small and fat.

Lon took out the tub of lime ice cream from his fridge. He handed the plastic tub up to me. I took the ice cream scooper he handed me and opened up the lid. Lon, down below, began to unbutton his shirt. I felt a wave of shame—what if someone walked in on this? What would my mom say? Or Stacey?

Now shirtless, Lon glanced up at me with a sly smile and lay down on the linoleum. His fat spread out laterally across his body, his chest and abdomen pink and tufted with hair. I thought of my dad—I hadn't seen him in five years but suddenly I missed him; I missed the feeling of lying on his chest as he read a story to me.

"I'm ready," Lon said.

I turned my attention to the vat of green, and scooped out a big spoonful. I held it in the air above Lon's body and laughed—this was going to be just like the slime drop on Nickelodeon. The ice cream dropped onto him and immediately began to melt—the green liquid seeping onto his armpits, his belly, his chest.

"Is that it?" he asked. "Is that all you want?"

"Yes," I said. I wanted it to be done. I felt like I'd taken a dare and now I really wanted to get out.

"You're a weird kid, Claire," he said, staring at me, half naked and covered in lime green sherbet. He stood up and walked down the hallway to his bathroom, and I could hear him turn on the shower.

I crawled down from the refrigerator and wiped my dusty hands off. I looked down the dark hallway and saw that he had left the bathroom door ajar. In that moment, I sensed what I would later learn for sure as an adult when I searched for Lon on the Internet and found his mug shot and a news story recounting his itinerant life as a chronic child molester: that there was something wrong with him and there was something wrong with our friendship. With that, I quickly opened his front door and ran outside to the parking lot in search of friends. I wanted to get away from the bad feeling, and fast.

CHAPTER EIGHT

On the Program

It was a cold night, the snow crunching under our feet. The moonlight shone through the splintery tree branches onto the gravel pathways that led from Utopia Park to the Maharishi Patanjali Golden Dome of Pure Knowledge. This was the men's dome—the grander of the two domes—and it was used for special occasions, although often men and women would sit separated. I hurried behind my mom and my brother who were walking fast, almost running. Around us, cars were backed up along the long block, waiting for parking spaces. A bicyclist, her body wrapped like a mummy in a long winter coat, swished past, ringing a little metallic bell as she went. Everyone seemed anxious about the time, hurrying to get to the dome before they blew the conch shell to mark the beginning of the festivities. If my memory is correct, it was January twelfth—Maharishi's birthday, and one of the biggest celebrations of the year.

Before us, the dome spread out like a giant golden spaceship, so big that I could barely see the other side of its magnificent arched roof. We joined the stream of people under the floodlights that marked the spectacular grand entrance. On either side of the red-carpeted gallery were two sweeping spiral staircases with arched wooden banisters. We began our ascent up into the flying hall. At the base of the stairs, the knobs atop the newel posts were solid gold, with images of the continents carefully raised on each sphere. I quickly ran my fingers across the curve of the Indian subcontinent before hurrying to catch up with my mom, allowing myself to imagine that I was on my way to a ball or a coronation. It all felt fairy-tale grand, which added to my sense of not belonging, of being an imposter, or at least a pauper. Looking around at the peacock spread of brilliant silk saris and brightly colored suits, I worried as always that my short-sleeved denim dress wasn't quite nice enough, or quite clean enough among such grandeur.

In we went, through the wide double doors to the grand flying hall. It felt like the innermost chamber of the palace. As far as the eye could see the floor was covered in foam, wrapped tightly in white sheets. People had set up their blankets and pillows and backpacks in careful lines, almost like tiny streets. I felt as if I had suddenly put on a space helmet as the sound of the thousands of hushed voices around us was muted by the huge arch of the room.

Stepping on the foam, I couldn't help but do a bouncing leap after my mom. She turned to give me a stern look, and I tried to keep it under control, following as she and Stacey turned to the right and plowed through the maze toward a group of friends.

Off to the side, along the shadowy perimeter, I saw mountains of extra foam piled high and a group of kids leaping through the air, pantomiming karate fights. Stacey pleaded to join them but my mom shook her head, and I worried that he would make her angry by whining or begging to go play. But then the sound of the conch shell silenced us.

The lights dimmed except for the few onstage. There I could

see various dignitaries and administrators sitting in high-backed golden chairs, all dressed in brilliant silk. Everyone closed their eyes for a group meditation. Leaning back, I heard the quiet rustle of several thousand people trying to be still. There was an excitement and intimacy about this silence that was unlike anything else.

"Jai Guru Dev," a reverent voice whispered into the microphone, and the lights brightened. On a large video screen on the side of the stage, Maharishi's face appeared above a large swarm of roses and poinsettias, and cries of joy rang out across the dome.

Before I knew it, I'd fallen asleep on the blankets, lulled by the warmth and the high, lilting sound of our guru's voice. I had no idea what he was saying, but I awakened to the sound of applause. Rubbing my eyes, I sat up and focused on the stage. A man in round glasses and a yellow suit was making an introduction. This is what I remember him saying:

"He's about to create the greatest adventure the world has ever known. He and Maharishi have spent hundreds of hours on this—he's going to give them the real glory and wonder! Dr. Doug Henning!"

Now I was wide awake. I loved Doug Henning! The long-haired elfin magician struck a glittering image in Fairfield with his handlebar mustache, his white suits, his beautiful wife, and his purple mansion. I had heard he was super famous—he had a TV show!—and he could supposedly do all sorts of wild things with special powers that Maharishi had helped give him.

He began with his dream. "A dream I had to create Maharishi Vedaland," Henning exclaimed, "a world-class theme park where you can actually take a trip through Maharishi's own consciousness." People laughed and rang their little golden bells. The idea of a magical meditation theme park was electrifying; most of them had been trying to take an extended trip through Maharishi's consciousness for over a decade.

I'd heard about the theme park when we first moved to Iowa, but it was supposed to be built in Fairfield. Now Henning had a set of poster boards set up on an easel and was describing a billion dollar attraction to be built on a huge swath of land maybe at Niagara Falls, maybe in Orlando, Florida, maybe in India too. He also said something about other countries too!

These would not be ordinary theme parks, Henning told us, speaking quickly, as if he couldn't get the words out fast enough. Maharishi had said, he told us gleefully, that his parks would make you Enlightened after you visited three times. This was a mind-boggling statement; Mom and everyone here had been meditating for years on end to become Enlightened. Could Maharishi just choose to make you Enlightened by having you visit a theme park? Why wouldn't he have done it before this? Henning slid in a new piece of poster board, showing a mountain with little trains around it.

"You get in a ride car and you go through the tunnel of awakening and you're given the complete mechanics of creation. We've created a completely silent room, [devoted to] Shiva. There's a golden glow, and you see the Vedic frequency. You go from self-referral to the whole of creation being manifested—Rishi, Devata, and Chandas. And subatomic particles start to appear. These molecules form, all the way on to the ever-expanding universe." Henning seemed wildly giddy and I felt myself caught up in the fantasy. Despite the fact that every adult I knew was pursuing Enlightenment, it didn't hold much personal sway over me. But magic and seeing the fabric of the universe? My mouth hung open as I listened. I needed to go to Vedaland.

"And then you see Maharishi in front of you and he says you are now entering your own consciousness!" The whole dome erupted in waves of laughter over the blissful image of Maharishi greeting you as a hologram. I didn't think it was that funny. Wasn't he basically a hologram now, hovering over us on projection screens, giggling and giving benedictions?

Henning continued to describe the park—the levitating pavilion, the golden chariot that would reduce you to the size of a quantum particle once you boarded it, the giant mountain ruled by the monkey god Hanuman who would swing you through the different levels of creation. There would be robots that looked like Dr. Brihaspati Dev Triguna, Maharishi's minister of health, and a mountain of immortality. There'd be a ride atop a giant golden bird that Henning said would cost $20 million to construct. In my mind, I was there, soaring through this park on this golden bird.

"The last step to Enlightenment," said Henning, "is a crystal-clear elevator that goes underwater to an ancient civilization that still lives in accord with Natural Law. You will get into old gondolas, and it will be an early morning of Vedic civilization. You'll see all the yogis on the banks, and they'll levitate in the air. It's the most beautiful thing you'll ever see."

Conch shells blew, bells rang, and we were all laughing. This would be absolutely the most incredible thing in the whole world. I wondered if as a Maharishi School student I might be eligible for some kind of summer job on the mountain of immortality. Henning told the excited crowd that the contractors for the theme park had become fast students of consciousness and Vedic literature, and everyone cheered as he described the head of construction—a neophyte to Maharishi's Knowledge—and his zealous passion for pursuing the guru's every wish. Now Henning paused dramatically.

He had everyone's attention. He said that *we* had raised only half the funding. It was up to all of us to work together, enlivening Nature Support to get the balance. Maharishi was confident that Nature Support would bring in the remaining hundreds of millions in the coming months.

I loved living in Utopia Park but I couldn't help but feel that Nature Support was more present in the lives of others—friends who got new toys, new clothes, ballet lessons, horseback-riding vacations, family vacations. When I complained to my mom, she would apologize to me, which just made me feel worse. "I'm doing my best, honey. Soon we are going to get some Nature Support and we can go somewhere amazing on vacation. Maybe you could even bring a friend." But watching my mom on a treadmill of work trying to make ends meet, I had started to lose faith. I was tired of willing Nature Support to notice us.

But this Vedaland project made me feel suddenly energized. After Henning left the stage, one of the university's scientists came to the microphone to talk about their newest research on the Maharishi Effect, quantum particles, and coherent consciousness. With Mom's weary permission, Stacey and I bounded through the shadowy aisles of adults listening raptly to the talk of quantum particles aligning. We made our way to the foam mountain and were immediately swept up in a Vedaland reenactment as gangs of kids from school pretended to be monkey gods and golden birds and robots. We didn't stop until we heard the bell ring to signal that they were serving cake, first placing slices in front of Maharishi and Guru Dev's photographs. This meant that outside the great hall there would be massive sheets of sugary white cake for the rest of us. We made our way back to Mom and out into the grand entrance, taking the little napkin full of white cake gratefully from a harried-looking server.

With the sweetness melting in our mouths, we made our way downstairs to put on our shoes and coats. The bracing cold of the dark night hit us as slim flakes of snow fell to the frozen ground. We made our way quietly back to Utopia Park, moving with the crowd, exhausted and eager to renew our efforts to get Nature Support.

There was always some new ambition of Maharishi's for which the community was asked to dig deeper and find a way to contribute so that his vision—our vision—of Heaven on Earth could be realized.

At school, we sang a new song at assemblies that trumpeted our dedication to using the Maharishi Effect to create World Peace:

Victory, before War!
No one's violating the laws of nature anymore!
Sound the triumphant horn! No enemy will be born!
We meditate and then create a positive permanent peaceful state
Victory before war!

We hadn't again achieved the magic Maharishi Effect number of seven thousand people flying together since the Taste of Utopia three years earlier. But there was social pressure to be on the Program in order to keep the dome numbers as high as possible. We needed 1,600 people meditating together daily to help create peace in the United States, and so there was a sense of duty. The movement had a department called the Global Good News, which reported how yogic flying, the group practice of TM, and even our own five-minute contribution of our Word of Wisdom was helping disarm Russia, bringing better weather to Africa, and bolstering the financial markets. Our school principal would boast about high attendance numbers on our morning announcements, correlating dome attendance and our school meditation to major world change.

People who were dedicated to the Program and working for the Movement exuded a sense of superiority. They were Governors of the Age of Enlightenment—which meant they had mastered Maharishi's advanced techniques—and they were single-minded in their dedication to helping Maharishi usher in the Age of Enlightenment.

Mom had worried about moving on campus; she thought we might have to dress differently and act more refined. Even though Mom loved Maharishi and loved meditating, she differentiated herself from the hard-core 'rus. She considered herself down to earth—she had to be. When she was at home, she liked to wear jeans (which were forbidden on campus) and T-shirts. It was rumored on campus that Maharishi had issued an edict back in the 1970s that he didn't like dark colors, and that we shouldn't dress in clothes darker than a leaf. Light colors, the story went, made people happy and dark colors invited negativity. Overnight all navy suits and brown dresses had vanished from the community. Since we understood that Maharishi's favorite color was gold, many of the high-level administrators chose this color for their wardrobe. The palette on campus was one of soft pinks, butter yellows, pale ivories, faded mint greens. The odd exception was our crisp formal navy winter uniforms—I guess the traditional look overcame the negativity. But it never made much sense.

*   *   *

Worse than wearing jeans and not enough pastel colors was that when Mom got mad or surprised, she could let her "fucks" and "shits" fly, loud and fast. Now that we were in Utopia Park, we felt like we couldn't be as loud or get in fights. If someone complained about us we could get kicked out, or Mom could get kicked out of the dome. The Capital of The Age of Enlightenment, the administrative office on campus that issued the entrance badges for the dome, was constantly withholding badge renewals for those whose behavior was considered not supportive of group consciousness.

Because of this, we were keenly aware of our neighbors. Across the street lived a childless couple. They weren't particularly interested in befriending us but focused their attentions on the small moneyed class of people who had moved to Fairfield with some form of independent wealth. Some had gained financial success elsewhere before coming to follow Maharishi's dream, but most of the well-off newcomers were supported by family wealth, parents or grandparents.

The most important benefactors in Fairfield at that time were the two Zimmerman brothers and their sister, whose married name was Chroman. Their father had started a chain of discount stores called Pic 'N' Save. These families were treated like royalty and in turn they gave Maharishi and his Movement substantial amounts of money. Maharishi even had a group of wealthy devotees called the "108s," which he had started in the seventies. (In Hinduism 108 is a sacred number; there are always 108 beads on a mala necklace, there are 108 names of Shiva, etc.) The 108s were allowed to live close to Maharishi in Europe and given nominal jobs in exchange for large donations. In Fairfield, there was the sense that the wealthy members of the Movement were further along in their evolutionary journey to Enlightenment and their wealth was due to great karma. Maharishi's inspirational slogan of living 200 percent of life—100 percent spiritual success and 100 percent material success—was repeated often in town as praise for those who were getting rich. Living 200 percent of life, as far as I could tell, meant being super-rich and also being on the Program.

Even as a kid, living in a spiritual community, it was very obvious to me who these people were. They always seemed to be dressed in the crisp pastel business casual separates that Maharishi endorsed—giving his Movement a corporate sheen. And at dome celebrations, they were always seated either in front of or on the stage. They were the best at following Maharishi's edict to live life effortlessly and were held up as ideals. They had the time to meditate for hours a day, doing the extra "rounds" of meditation that accelerated spiritual Enlightenment. They could afford the special conferences and retreats that Maharishi held around the world. And then they could spend the rest of their time volunteering on the many committees and boards that helped the university function. Above all, the wealthy had access to Maharishi—they could visit him in his outposts outside the U.S. and return with the newest quotes and ideas on how to live ideally.

In my class, there was a clear divide between those whose parents had come to Fairfield with resources and those who hadn't. After a few years at the school, I now had a best friend named Genevra. Genevra's father had a successful company before moving to Fairfield, and when the family arrived they bought one of the town's most elegant properties—a large gabled mansion that sat on acres of rolling hills, perfectly perched on the main thoroughfare. Genevra was the only one of us with a pool, and I was always angling to spend more time at her house. Sleepovers at Genevra's place were an enchanted time for me as we wandered from room to room, each one perfectly done in a single color—bright pink, mint green. There were silhouetted portraits of Genevra and her little brother, and family photographs in the den.

We would play dolls on the long swath of her purple-carpeted bedroom, and open her whitewashed wooden blinds to look out at her estate. I would see her mom, a small pink turban on her head, talking on the phone to the school committee about the latest fund-raiser. On the weekends, as the sun started to disappear behind the horizon, there was always the inevitable call from her mother: "Girls, it's time to meditate." We would trudge away and do as we were told, giggling as we tried to keep silent.

I deeply admired and coveted all of Genevra's and her family's life. They were so obviously living 200 percent of Life.

When I first started at the Maharishi School, there had been a constant influx of new students as families came in and out of Fairfield, testing the idea of living in the Dawn of the Age of Enlightenment. But, over the years, that influx had slowed and stabilized into a close-knit class of thirteen girls. We knew each other's strengths and weaknesses. I was, for example, tied for the position of the fastest reader with another girl named Jenny, whose birthday was three weeks after mine. But I was low on the totem pole when it came to sports, usually picked second to last, just before a girl who was a foot shorter than the rest of us. We played our roles steadfastly, rarely challenging one another's territory. Joey was great at art; her best friend Ingrid was a budding cellist and also very good at math. Both of them had parents heavily involved with the school. Joey's mom was a trustee and Ingrid's father was one of the deans of the university. Nadia and Orpita both lived in Utopia Park like me. Gina's father was the principal and her birthday was just a few days away from Joey's.

I awaited my own birthday with a particular eagerness. At ten years of age, I would be old enough to receive my sitting technique. This would be my real initiation into TM—and a real dividing line. I felt the Word of Wisdom, the mantra I'd received as a three-year-old, was for the babies, a soft little practice you could do while coloring or walking around. But getting your sitting technique meant that you were now grouped with the adults. The sitting technique was what my mom and all her friends had been taught in college back in the seventies, and what had changed their lives so dramatically. It meant that you closed your eyes, that you sat still for ten minutes, and that you connected more deeply to the Unified Field of All Consciousness.

At the beginning of fourth grade, when we were all nine years old, we were told to split into two groups to begin to learn the mechanics of Transcendental Meditation. I was put into the older group—being born in March, I was the youngest. This meant in the fall, we would be excused from morning SCI class and be taken across campus to the local TM Center. It was situated in the three-story buildings near the domes, called the "high-rises,"which urban transplants to our low-lying town always said with a smile. Inside the TM Center, there was the hushed and gilded reverent atmosphere of the dome—golden walls and furniture, red carpet— but the mood was somewhat corporate. On our first day, we were greeted by a slight man who wore the requisite pale suit; he seemed strangely nervous or intimidated by the six of us. We were directed to a set of folding chairs and at the front of the room was a foldout metal easel with a large white pad of drawing paper on it.

The man began to talk about how the universe was like an ocean, an ocean of consciousness. This sounded familiar to me but I had never had anyone explain it concisely. The inside of our minds was a giant ocean of all being and, when we quietly said our supersecret TM mantra, our consciousness would drop like a stone to the bottom of this great ocean. This was the deepest state of consciousness, but more important, the source of all being; by diving way down there we could harvest endless creativity.

It sounded amazing. Lately, my Word of Wisdom hadn't been doing much for me and, at school, I usually found myself lost in thought for the five minutes or so when we were supposed to be chanting inside our heads. I'd think about my mom and worry about whether she would have enough money for rent, and before I knew it, meditation time was over, and I was more anxious than I had been before.

Once the TM teacher had finished talking about consciousness, he said we could ask questions. Six hands shot up in the air. He looked petrified as we began to interrupt each other. "Can we sing our mantra to the tune of our favorite song?" "Can we whisper it out loud if we are alone?" "What if I forget my mantra?" "What if I get sleepy?"

With my big initiation coming up, my mom bought me a crisp new cotton lilac-striped dress, and we went to the grocery store to get fruit and flowers, just as we had done in Manhattan six years before.

On the appointed Saturday morning, a few days after my tenth birthday, Mom and I got into our station wagon and drove to the

TM Center. The sky outside was a pale white and the trees were leaf-less silhouettes on the horizon, the ground still frozen from the long winter. The TM Center was quiet. Inside, we were greeted by Mom's friend Nancy. Nancy was a fair-skinned, soft-spoken lady who favored prairie dresses and seemed intent on embodying Maharishi's vision of nurturing as the core female virtue. I'd babysat for her toddler son a few times while Nancy meditated in the other room. And I knew that she'd lost her first child when her husband accidentally backed his truck over the boy in the driveway. This tragedy, along with her being my mother's employer, gave Nancy an air of sad authority that I respected. That morning I felt almost trancelike as she asked in her lilting voice if I was ready to be initiated.

She asked me back to a small room, where two chairs sat facing a picture of Guru Dev. Incense was burning and we kneeled in front of the picture while Nancy rattled off a long list of Sanskrit words—names of the many gods who had helped us to meditate. When it was over, we sat in the chairs facing each other, and I felt really grown up. She told me my new mantra, which was a slightly different monosyllabic sound than my Word of Wisdom. I said it silently to myself. It was shorter than my other mantra, and I felt like I was dropping down inside my head, almost as if I was descending in an elevator with my eyes closed. Nancy whispered for me to say it for ten minutes and stepped out of the room.

My new mantra actually did take me deeper inside myself. It was a quiet feeling—not scary, but comforting. When Nancy came back and whispered, "Jai Guru Dev," I slowly opened my eyes, blinking as I took in the golden furniture around me. I smiled, big. "Was it easy?" she asked. I nodded. "Was it good?" I nodded again. I had a real TM mantra and I felt a little closer to what all the adults around me had been experiencing.

My dad, his brother, and their father *(from left to right)*. Dad would often regale us with dark stories of the Hoffman family curse—alcoholism, suicide, and crime.

My mom in Boulder at the University of Colorado in the late sixties, around the time that she first learned Transcendental Meditation and met Maharishi Mahesh Yogi.

My parents on their wedding day in 1974. They had met and fallen in love at a Transcendental Meditation retreat that year.

An undated photo of my dad carrying me, my brother Stacey clinging to his leg. Struggling with alcoholism, Dad disappeared when I was five years old.

An undated photo of the campus of Maharishi International University. In the dome-shaped buildings in the background, group meditations took place each day, with thousands of people practicing the trademarked "flying program."

With Stacey shortly after we arrived in Fairfield. Unable to afford the private school for meditators, we had to tough it out with the townies at public school.

Standing next to Stacey on our first day at the Maharishi School of the Age of Enlightenment, where students learned Maharishi's philosophy for living and practiced group meditations.

Me with my baton-twirling team performing at the Golden Domes.
Dome celebrations often featured telecasts of Maharishi speaking from India.

With my meditation teacher in Utopia Park on the day I learned my
"sitting technique" meditation, around my tenth birthday.

Me, age fifteen, in my dad's apartment in Los Angeles, surrounded by his artwork. Life in L.A. with Dad was a stark contrast to the utopian community back in Iowa.

Left: Me, Stacey, and Mom in the early 1990s. It was during this time that Stacey and I began to rebel against the community's pursuit of Enlightenment. *Right:* Me at sixteen. I often snuck out of the trailer in Utopia Park to go to hog roasts and bonfires while my family slept.

Photo of the Golden Dome after a snowfall. In recent years attendance has dropped from the thousands who gathered there in the '80s to meditate. *Photo by Stacey Hoffman*

In between the two Golden Domes stands Maharishi's Tower of Invincibility, a little-used structure that is illuminated at night to celebrate one of Maharishi's ideal qualities. *Photo by Stacey Hoffman*

Stacey and me
on my wedding
day in 2009 in
Los Angeles.

With Mom and
Stacey in early 2008
near Utopia Park.
Maharishi died the
following month.

*   *   *

One evening, Mom came home from the dome with a funny look on her face and big news. Maharishi had decided that he would show the world what he had for so long kept secret: Flying! And it wasn't just going to be people flying in front of us—they were going to have a competition.

Mom wasn't as excited as we were—I guessed because she saw people fly every day in the dome—but Stacey and I were buzzing around the house, imagining what we were going to see. Would they fly all the way across the dome? How would they stop once they started?

Mom tried to settle us down and tell us that there were actually three stages of flying: hopping, hovering, and flying.

"I'm still at the hopping phase," she said. "Most of the people in the dome are in the hopping phase. Although some people are really good, they can really move across the foam." She laughed, but this didn't seem that funny to me. People weren't flying?

Had anyone hovered? Did Maharishi hover? I asked. "I'm not sure, honey. I've seen paintings from the past of great sages who could levitate, but I don't think anyone is doing it now. I would think Maharishi could do it, but he hasn't shown it."

This was puzzling information to me, as I'd imagined in all the secrecy surrounding the dome that out-of-this-world things were happening inside. Why would my mom spend so much time there if she had just been hopping around for hours? And why would we have endured all the townies yelling names at us if we weren't really flying?

Mom assured me that hopping was pretty incredible, and that it defied the laws of physics. That it was a totally effortless motion that happened because people were connecting with the Unified Field.

But the next morning when we drove past the Golden Domes, I couldn't look at them in quite the same way, knowing that people weren't zooming through the air inside.

A few weeks later, on a spring day, Ms. Onasch had all the lower-school classes line up outside in the yard. Our classes had been split by gender the year before and we rarely joined the boys for school events. Maharishi said this helped boys and girls reach their full potential with less distraction, and it helped accelerate the process of Enlightenment. I studied the boys carefully. They were fighting and pushing each other. Some hung back, eyes cast to the ground. Brendan, a dark-haired, deep-eyed boy who had been at the school since kindergarten and recently had become obsessed with American Indians, ran up to the girls' line and did an Apache whoop. We all screamed and grabbed each other, laughing till Ms. Onasch quieted us down.

Ms. Onasch was tall, with an hourglass figure that she accentuated with fitted cashmere turtlenecks and knee-length skirts. Unlike the other teachers, she didn't seem to care for pastels. She wore vibrant reds and oranges and fuchsias and we swarmed around her like hummingbirds. She was from South America, and she said she grew up speaking Spanish, so she took it upon herself to teach us some. This was a welcome break from SCI—every subject we studied at school quickly became about Maharishi's principles of living. But with Spanish, there was no space for philosophy.

The school principal, Mr. Orange, walked past our squealing lines, his tall frame tilted forward, dressed in a crisp beige three-piece suit. We calmed down as he called us to attention, his voice booming across the yard. "Jai Guru Dev, students. May I have your attention please? We are going to the Maharishi Pantajali Dome, the men's dome, to watch a Yogic Flying demonstration. I want you to be on your very best behavior. You are the future leaders of the Age of Enlightenment, and I want each of you to be representative of Maharishi's teaching. Today is a great day and I want everyone to understand the importance of it." We stared at him. "Let's go," he said.

With a decisive turn, in a hushed silence, he led the classes up the hill along the cracked sidewalk that led past the Chapel, an eighty-year-old structure built of large white stones in the Gothic style. Massive stained glass windows lined the sides, with beautiful ancient-looking figures acting out scenes I didn't understand. Men wore robes and released doves. Angels floated above hilltops. As I carefully avoided the cracks in the sidewalk and listened to the kids around me talking about Yogic Flying, I wondered if angels really flew, or if they too were maybe just hopping around.

Inside the dome, we bounced along the foam and sat in groups according to grade. This was an exhibition just for Maharishi School students, and there was a buzz in the air. We sat close to the front of the dome, where the stage was. I'd never been this close before and I felt sort of important as I sat down.

A long rectangular stretch of foam had been cordoned off in front of the stage with white string and little sticks, giving it the look of a miniature runway. On one end, a group of about five men were sitting in the lotus position on a higher pile of foam. They wore pastel scrub pants—like doctors—and light colored T-shirts. I recognized one guy—his daughter was at the Maharishi School—and I felt thankful that my mom wasn't demonstrating Yogic Flying for us.

From out of nowhere, Bevan Morris appeared and we all fell silent. "Jai Guru Dev, students!" he said, his voice quivering with excitement. "We are so fortunate today to share with you Maharishi's TM-Siddhi program and get a chance for all of you to see what your parents have been enjoying for all these years."

Bevan tittered at his own joke and our teachers laughed along with him. I didn't hear much more of what he said because I was focused on the men on the foam. They had closed their eyes now, their faces going completely still. One of them was swaying ever so slightly back and forth. Bevan finished his introduction—something about how they'd done a demonstration in Washington, D.C., and how the world's press had been awed by the feats of Maharishi's Yogic Flyers. And then there was silence. Bevan rang a small brass bell to mark the beginning of the competition.

I leaned forward to see, trying to maneuver around all the other kids craning to get a glance. Nothing was happening. The men were sitting there in the lotus position, their legs folded like pretzels. I had my eye on the one whose body was slightly swaying from side to side—I thought he'd be the first to go.

In that instant, a man in a light blue shirt bounced off the foam pile and made two short hops down the runway. He'd just sort of exploded, like a kernel of corn popping, his butt briefly lifting off the foam as he bounced forward. The other men came afterward and all of a sudden there were five men on the runway, bouncing forward. Their bodies were lean as they hopped along, their eyes closed as if lost in deep meditation. Our teachers were quietly oohing and ahhing—these men were supposed to be the best Yogic Flyers in the Movement. And then it was over. They all reached the end of the runway in a little cluster. I couldn't see who had won. But I didn't care. It all felt very weird to me.

Why were they competing at meditation? It had looked different from anything I'd seen before—it was not the hovering across the floor that I'd imagined—and it was definitely strange. It felt like we were celebrating something that didn't totally make sense. Our teachers rang little bells to celebrate the finish of the race. The men lined up again. They were going to do hurdles now, hopping over little piles of foam. Around me kids were starting to whisper to each other but I didn't want to think about what was going on anymore. It felt sort of impolite to watch the intense bodily movements. I scooted to the edge of our group and lay my head down on the foam and closed my eyes. I said my mantra to myself, trying to push away my confusion.

CHAPTER NINE

200 Percent of Life

All around us, other parents were pulling into the long circular driveway of the Maharishi School and dropping off kids before the nine-thirty bell. I saw a few of my friends from my fifth-grade class racing toward the door. To me they all seemed to be yelling and shouting: happy families, unembarrassed. We on the other hand were silent as my brother opened the squeaky car door and climbed out into the gray slush that coated the street. He muttered an obligatory thank you and tromped up the sidewalk, not looking back. His jacket was stained, duct tape holding together a tear in the back.

It was the end of winter. Mom had woken us up that morning by clanging in the kitchen, an alarm bell of guilt that quickly jostled me out of bed. I knew I needed to be pitching in more. School didn't start until nine thirty, but Mom had just come home from the dome where she did her morning meditation and found us still asleep. We were supposed to do our chores and eat breakfast together before we left the house in our uniforms. Mom had carefully drawn the chore chart on a long sheet of paper with ruler-lined grids, and it was now the focus of every morning. Jeff and her friends had always teased her about her occasionally strict demeanor with us, calling her "Sergeant Liz." With Mom working all the time, we were seeing more and more of Sergeant Liz these days. Stacey and I had two chores each to do—put away the dishes from the rack and sweep the kitchen floor. Lately tensions had escalated around the chart.

Whenever we forgot to do stuff, we were quickly reminded of how much Mom was working and how we needed to do our part.

I pushed off my flowered polyester comforter, burned in spots where my lightbulb had scorched the fabric as I had buried myself under the covers to read late into the night. On the wall above me, I had carefully taped up a poster of Marilyn Monroe. Mom had frowned when I picked it out but I loved Marilyn and had developed a rapturous fixation on her. I pushed open the flimsy metal frame door of my closet. The wallpaper was stripped and faded, the old brown flowers peeling off in spots where the furniture had bumped up against it. When I had walked into it the first time, and seen the brown flowers on the wall and the beige carpet, it had seemed elegant, empty and clean. Now it was crowded with the junk of my adolescence. I had an old wooden vanity that Mom had gotten me for my birthday, with a triptych of mirrors that I used to gaze at myself from all angles. It was covered in pictures of models and actresses I'd torn out of magazines. They were edgy and stylish—things I yearned to be but was definitely not.

I opened the closet and pulled out my uniform: a rumpled wool jumper and a graying, white Peter Pan blouse. I buttoned up my shirt and strained to pull the thinning wool jumper over my head. I'd always been a skinny, asthmatic kid, but lately my chest was expanding rapidly. My body pushed against the dress. There were girls in my class who had started wearing training bras but this didn't look anything like boobs to me. It was a thickness that, coupled with my round face, was starting to look a lot like fat. I reached into a drawer, pushing aside my small hidden journal and found my red bow tie. When I started going to the Maharishi School of the Age of Enlightenment, it had been a dream come true, and this uniform, this bow tie had been a badge of belonging that I had been so thrilled to wear. Now the tie was worn from years of use, and stained with ghee and tofu.

In the kitchen, I found Stacey and Mom arguing—he hadn't finished his project for his seventh-grade SCI course and he hadn't put his tie on and he hadn't taken a shower. This morning he was not embodying any of Maharishi's Sixteen Values of Creative Intelligence that were listed on the mimeographed sheet of paper his teacher had given him, most obviously

Active, *takes a*
Direction *toward*
Progress, *and*
Transcending,
Accelerates *the*
Integration *of*
Stability *and*
Adaptability, *and*
Enjoys
Evolution

And Mom was pissed, murmuring about how she was fed up with his bad attitude. Mom had a temper that she mostly tried to control. She would tell us about how awful her own mother had been—throwing food at her, screaming at her for reasons unknown. We knew she was trying to be a better parent to us than what she'd grown up with. But sometimes, it felt like an alter ego would emerge and my mom would become livid with anger, shouting strange oldfangled things like "Shit, piss, and corruption," and looking at us with utter contempt.

We climbed into our rusted, wood-grained Pinto, Mom turned the key, and the engine sputtered and spat until it finally turned over. The car was freezing—underneath the front floorboards, a large hole had rusted out that winter, and even though Mom had put mats down, it was impossible for the car to get warm, and the smell of gasoline was overwhelming. Mom and Stacey began arguing again and I looked out at the snow-covered campus and tuned them out, trying to imagine myself as a fifties starlet being transported from my penthouse to a luncheon.

As we turned onto Zimmerman Boulevard, I saw a group of angry-looking people standing next to the entrance of campus, holding signs. "Hindu Cult," "Transcendental Meditation Is a Cult!" "Maharishi Brainwashes Followers."

I read the signs quickly, slightly terrified by the jagged hand lettering.

"Mom," I asked, "what is brainwashing?" I imagined someone pouring water into my ears, then sloshing it around.

She turned to look at the protesters, and then sped up, her face uneasy. "Those people are insane, Claire. Ignore them. Stay away from them."

Mom reached back and pushed the seat forward to let me out of the back. The Pinto shuddered and stalled, and I looked around to see if anyone had noticed. I gave her a cautious smile, but she was staring forward, her shiny brown hair creating a mask around her face. She was still angry. I reached across the old cracked pleather seats and gave Mom a hug. Underneath her snowy boots, I saw the hole in the floorboard by the driver's pedal. Through the open wound of the rotting metal, the dirty snow of the street was just inches away.

"I'll see you at lunchtime," she grumbled.

It was around this time that I began to see cracks in the Heaven on Earth realm we'd been living in. My brother had watched his friend's father, Ed Beckley, fall apart after his Millionaire Maker program filed for bankruptcy in 1987. Ed was unable to make good on the money-back guarantee demands from the 40,000 customers who had paid $295 for his get-rich-quick program. Nearly all of his 560 employees were fired. (Later Ed was sentenced to federal prison for wire fraud.)

The First Age of Enlightenment Credit Union went into receivership in 1985 after it became overextended. A local "Siddha-owned" oil brokerage firm in Fairfield was ordered to pay over $100,000 in damages to an employee who said he was fired after driving a "rival guru" to the airport.

In 1989 International Trading Group Ltd. filed for bankruptcy after federal regulators accused the commodity firm of bilking investors of more than $450 million. The Fairfield office was, in those final years before it went bust, reportedly the top money producer for the national firm, according to the *Chicago Tribune*. Now it was closed and many of the meditators who worked there were scrambling to find other jobs.

When I was in sixth grade, Maharishi decided that we would become experts in something called Vedic Math. One morning, we all lined up, then headed outside under a flat gray sky, the wind cutting across the open plains with a wicked bite. The girls around me fell off into small groups, and I found myself walking to the side, preoccupied with my own thoughts.

In my pocket, I had a vial of lip gloss that I had talked my mom into buying for me at the drugstore. It was called Kissing Potion, a name that I found totally humiliating, but I was too interested in the wet look that it offered to let the name put me off. I whipped out the small, clear tube and ran a dab over my lips, then stashed the tube away before anyone could catch me preening. Across the meadow, the boys' class was walking toward us, led by their teacher Mrs. Greenley.

We met at the center of the field, and I stared down at the ground, avoiding eye contact with any of the boys. Mrs. Greenley and our teacher Mrs. Hall greeted each other with a perfunctory "Jai Guru Dev" and traded groups. Some of the bolder, early-breasted girls had made friends with the boys and they said hello to each other in a sophisticated and enviable way.

We followed Mrs. Greenley the rest of the way up the hill into her classroom. She was my least favorite teacher, the mother of my least favorite classmate, Erin. The sixth-grade boys' classroom was on the opposite side of the lawn from ours. With its high wood ceilings and dark green indoor/outdoor carpeting, it had been the TV lounge for the old Parsons College dorms, and it retained a slightly seedy, dank smell. As we filed in, Mrs. Greenley told us to go find a spot in the corner for guided meditation.

I sat down at a desk, feeling anxious. Math was a subject that had never particularly challenged me until this year. I had a robust memory and had easily memorized all the multiplication tables. Mom was good at math, and said it was in our genes. "Your grandfather is an engineer, you can do this," she would say when helping with my homework. It seemed to work—until that fall.

We had been told that Vedic Math would be blissful for us but it hadn't been for me. The computational methods were based on sixteen sutras that are directly derived from Atharva-Veda, one of the four main branches of ancient Vedic literature. Our teacher told us that Vedic Math made everything easier by replacing large numbers with small numbers and breaking computations down into simple steps that you could do in your head. She also said that Maharishi had said the practice of Vedic Mathematics helped to create a general state of awareness, while at the same time focusing on a specific point. Cultivating that ability to maintain the wholeness while focusing on the parts of knowledge, he said, would allow us to live (even more?) in accord with Natural Law.

How did it work? For example, to multiply, you used the third sutra, Urdhva Tiryagbhaym, which meant "vertically and crosswise." A sutra was just like a mantra, but instead of a sound, it had a meaning. Instead of doing 33 x 12, you would use the "unit digits" 3 and 2, multiply them and get the number six. That was the vertical answer. Then, Mrs. Greenley said, the units digit of each number is multiplied by the tens digit of the other number and these two numbers are added. I was bleary eyed at this point—were we still talking about numbers or was this an SCI lesson with some hidden philosophical message?

Mrs. Greenley continued, writing on the board. The crosswise multiplication would give the answer: (2 x 3) + (3 x 1) = 9. Nine, she said, was the tens digit of the answer. Then the two tens digits are multiplied, vertically, to get the hundreds digit of the answer, three. Three, nine, six! She wrote out the numbers on the board, and it was as if she had completed a magic trick. It seemed more complicated to me than it needed to be, but Mrs. Greenley insisted that we show our work on the page. For guidance, she had hung a long handmade banner on the wall, next to Maharishi's principles of SCI, which listed the sixteen sutras.

"Even young children take delight in this approach to mathematical problems. Their faces shine with joy and amazement as they learn to add, subtract, multiply, and divide," one of the math teachers was quoted as saying in an article about Vedic Math in the school newsletter. "Often the children burst into peals of laughter as they quickly move through long rows of previously tedious computation."

As for me, I was utterly confused by even basic questions of multiplication. Although the Vedas were credited as the basis for all of the Knowledge that our Movement followed, we didn't actually read any of them. Instead, our knowledge came from Maharishi's Enlightened illumination and translation of them. The way my teachers explained it, he was able to bypass the extra stuff that Hindus and Indian civilization had layered on over the centuries, motivated by human history and greed. Maharishi's translation of the Vedas was essential and pure.

Living in Iowa in the 1980s, it seemed that Maharishi seemed intent on making Fairfield—and our lives here—more closely resemble the ideal ancient Vedic civilization he was always envisioning.

Sometimes this brought true blessings, at least if you were a kid. That year, word was sent down that—in order to have a more blissful Vedic family experience—we should have a two-hour lunch break during the school day. Our teachers had seemed a little stunned when they delivered this news to us, perhaps wondering where that extra hour of class time was going to come from. Mom wasn't thrilled either—there was panic in her voice when she got the sheet from school. "What am I supposed to tell them at work?" she asked. "I get paid by the hour! That's two less hours!"

I was, however, thrilled, because we were spending less and less time doing actual schoolwork. After all, work was effort and life was meant to be effortless. The school administrators argued that we didn't need as much "time on task" since our consciousness was being raised by Maharishi's programs.

Science, Maharishi said, was the language of the West. In order for Americans to understand something, it had to be scientific. On the walls of our classrooms and everywhere you looked on the Maharishi university campus, there were elaborate charts and diagrams showing how Maharishi's interpretation of Vedic knowledge was scientific. What did "scientific" mean? It meant that you could prove that Maharishi was right. There were laboratories on campus where scientists worked for years, proving that Maharishi's Knowledge was scientifically accurate. More and more, Maharishi's Vedic Knowledge seemed to be flowing into our community at an unstoppable pace, codifying every aspect of life.

But the Vedic science that came to monopolize our lives was Maharishi's Ayurveda, his interpretation of the ancient Vedic science of health and the body. Overnight, Ayurveda became the organizing principal of how members of our community looked at themselves and the way they lived their lives.

According to Ayurveda, there are three different body types, or doshas—Vata, Pitta, and Kapha. These correspond, respectively, to air and space, fire and water, and earth and water. Maharishi didn't want us just to understand our individual doshas but encouraged us to see the whole world according to this division. There were Vata, Pitta, and Kapha times of days, seasons, qualities, tastes, and so on.

Maharishi sent doctors from India to come to Fairfield and visit the Maharishi School. A creaky old Indian man named Dr. Triguna taught us how to take our own pulses and diagnose any imbalances in our doshas. A handsome young doctor named Deepak Chopra, who we were told was Maharishi's personal physician, came and talked to us about meditation and physiology. At a school assembly, he also lectured us on balancing our doshas to connect with the Unified Field. Everything was about curing imbalance, smoothing out any physiological irregularities so that we could be a perfect reflection of the Laws of Nature.

Now, every moment of every day had a prescription from Maharishi on how to be and how to act. According to Ayurveda, one should awaken at six o'clock in the morning so as best to align oneself with the rhythms of nature.

Instead of rolling out of bed and taking a shower, we were meant to give ourselves a full body massage—an abhyanga—using Maharishi Ayurveda oils (also chosen according to our specific body constitution or dosha). This was followed by tongue scraping, gargling with oils, body scrubbing, copious herb taking, and then of course asanas, pranayama—breathing techniques—and finally a lengthy meditation.

Maharishi Gandharva Vedic music was the sound track we were supposed to play throughout these lengthy prescribed rituals. We were told it was to be kept playing in empty rooms when you weren't there in order to balance the energy of your living space. The wiry sound of the sitar, the pounding of the tabla, the tinkling keys of the santoor—this was a constant backdrop wherever I went—coming from small CD players in empty rooms set to play the healing sounds on a loop. The music was selected according to the season and the time of day, again, to be better aligned with nature.

Even at school, before our twice-daily meditations, we had to do asanas, and then pranayama breathing, and then five minutes of taking our pulse to balance our doshas. Lunchtime was equally ritualistic. The lunch hall was filled with people who were in the midst of a popular Ayurvedic cleanse—panchakarma—which required them to get daily enemas, eat a strict and spare diet, and take lots of herbs along with spoonfuls of ghee, or clarified butter. They received hours-long oil massages at the Maharishi Ayurveda Clinic that had opened on the edge of campus, and soon it felt like every meditator had a slightly greasy sheen. The women wore soft pastel-colored turbans to hide their oil-soaked hair. Those turbans became a status symbol of sorts—these women were aggressively pursuing Enlightenment.

After our two-hour Vedic lunch break, we'd read from the Rig Veda in history class. In the afternoon, we had thirty minutes allotted to listen to Maharishi Gandharva Veda, which Maharishi said would raise our IQs just by the sound of a CD of his trademarked sitar and tabla music. We started taking Gandharva Vedic music classes once a week. I plucked away halfheartedly at a sitar with an old Indian man who spoke almost no English and seemed vaguely contemptuous both of us and of rural Iowa. Sanskrit, first introduced during our SCI classes as a way to get closer to the Ved, would become a language requirement. In science, we'd learn about how Maharishi's principles were clearly illustrated even in the process of photosynthesis—Life Is Found in Layers, Inner Depends on Outer.

Our school play that year was also based on Maharishi's principles. Each elementary school kid would shout one of these principles after acting out one aspect of nature's perfection. The kids in overalls, dressed as farmers, plowed the "Field of All Possibilities," because as Maharishi said, "The Field of All Possibilities Is the

Source of All Solutions." I was assigned the role of a Southern belle, and was part of a group of about eight girls who waltzed across the stage, wearing gingham dresses and singing in a high falsetto about the wonders of such a perfectly functioning world. "How do the waves know when to wash to the shore," we sang along, making a feminine little frame around our faces as instructed. "Oh what a bright, bright, intelligent world we live in!"

Positivity was paramount at the Maharishi School. We were told to always focus on the blissful aspect of life, and avoid negativity. One day, Mom got a call from one of Stacey's teachers, reporting that he had been drawing monsters in art class. Monsters were not part of Bliss Consciousness. They suggested maybe Stacey might be un-stressing and needed some guidance. Mom pushed back—there were few areas that held higher ground for her than Maharishi's Knowledge, and art was one of them. Stacey had been drawing monsters for as long as I could remember and Mom encouraged him as he developed them as googly-eyed, long-finger-nailed characters. "Keep drawing the monsters, Stacey," she told him. "But maybe just draw them at home."

It felt funny to have Mom disagree with the school, but I liked it. It made me feel as if Mom liked us the way we were. But it also gave me a twinge of anxiety—why did we have to act different at school?

The Maharishi School newsletter that came home in my backpack reported to parents an eclectic mix of Iowan and Vedic education. Amid the list of class parent contacts and information about a barn raising and PTA meetings were columns headed "The Ministry of Education and Enlightenment," and "The Ministry of Development of Consciousness." Under "The Ministry of Health and Immortality and Ministry of Natural Law and Order," families of school-age children were informed that "of the many topics that these two ministries encompass, orderliness, safety, and health stand out. As we prepare for our children to return to school the following areas demand the more immediate attention . . ." What followed were classes on Enlightened discipline, Ayurvedic health care for children, head lice guidelines, and Maharishi's views on water purity.

"Did you know," the newsletter asked, "our collective group consciousness will create Heaven in our school and therefore Heaven on Earth?"

By 1998, every school assembly and dome celebration meant an unveiling of some new and vital Knowledge from Maharishi. After conch shells were blown and the administrators made their speeches, the giant projection screens would unfurl from around the front perimeter of the dome. A hushed silence would fall as the image of Maharishi would flicker to life on the screen. It was always the same setup—him sitting on a silky dais, wrapped in white robes, surrounded by flowers. At the start, he was always meditating, his eyes closed. He seemed totally unaware of the thousands gazing at him on the other side of the world. And then his eyes would open. He'd blink and look around at whoever was near him in that faraway remote place. And like clockwork he would let out a gleeful sort of giggle.

Inevitably, there in the dome or the assembly hall, that giggle would be contagious, echoing through the crowd, everyone laughing along with Maharishi's laughter. I guess that imagining what the world looked like through his Enlightened reality, possessing total knowledge of the universe, was funny. His laughter made us all feel that our concerns and anxieties were illusions. That life, as Maharishi said, was pure unbounded bliss.

And the amazing thing was, we were chosen to live this bliss. This was our dharma—our right path. Our karma had led us here, our teachers told us, led us to be a part of the Dawn of the Age of Enlightenment. Every day we were reminded that we, the children of Siddhas, students of the Maharishi School, were Brahmin— reincarnated. We were a blessed tribe of ancient Indian Enlightened sages who had chosen to be reborn at this moment in time as we stood on the precipice of World Peace. Was it too good to be true?

PART TWO

Doubting

CHAPTER TEN

Dad Comes Home

Out of the blue, a letter arrived in the mail from Dad. I was eleven years old and I hadn't heard a word from him in almost six years. My mother, brother, and I never spoke of him at home. He had abandoned us, so the best we could do was erase him from our lives. I had gotten used to the familiar stutter that my teachers or other parents made when they began a statement with, "Your Mom and Dad . . . ," quickly stifling the last part of the phrase. On Father's Day, Stacey and I would make cards for my mom, declaring her the Best Mom Ever, and she would accept them with a rueful smile. I'd even told most of my friends that he was dead; it was easier than explaining what had really happened.

On the day the letter came, my mom stood frozen, staring at the envelope, in front of the row of metal mailboxes near the entrance of Utopia Park. I knew immediately something was wrong. Despite all the meditating, I was still an anxious kid, and I watched my mom like a hawk. Between our moves around the country and my mom's treadmill of part-time jobs, I always kept my eyes open for the next thing that would throw our life back into chaos. Recently, at the health food store, I'd picked up a bottle of herbal supplements near the register that said they "eased anxiety," which sounded really good to me. I felt as though I had too many thoughts running through my head all the time—it wasn't at all the transcendental silence that Maharishi described. But when I asked Mom to buy them for me, she frowned and put them back. "You don't need this," she said. "Do you?"

"I guess not," I replied. And then I felt embarrassed and, well, a little anxious about it.

That spring day, Mom grabbed the rest of the mail, walked back to the station wagon, and placed the long, thick envelope on the tattered center console. It was addressed to Stacey and me in my father's wild, all-capitals scrawl. She turned the key in the ignition and the Pinto stuttered and stalled. She stared ahead, her whole face weighed down by sadness. I felt my stomach turn over and I closed my eyes and tried to focus on making the engine turn over. She tried again and it started.

We drove home in silence. Mom took the letter into her bedroom, dragging the phone in with her. I could hear her crying as she asked her brassy best friend Courtenay for advice on what to do. Courtenay had gotten married the year before and so she spent less time at our kitchen table with Mom. But she was still my mom's first phone call in a crisis, especially when it came to men.

Stacey and I puttered around the living room waiting to see the letter. A little later, Mom called us into her bedroom. Her face was wet and blotchy and she seemed oddly ceremonial. We sat down heavily on her bed, staring at the wall as she read aloud to us from the pages of the yellow steno paper.

"It's your Dad/Fred," he wrote. "I have missed you more than you will ever know." He admitted that he was an alcoholic and that he had joined Alcoholics Anonymous and that he was now sober.

This letter, he told us, was the first step in a process called "making amends." He explained that he wanted to come back into our lives, to be near us, to be our dad again. He wanted our forgiveness. He said that he knew this must've been painful for us but that whatever we felt, it had been even worse for him. Listening to my mother's voice quiver, her eyes damp, I felt strangely empty. I didn't want to hear about my father's hurt or pain or think about my own—I'd been keeping that far away. I just wanted to see him, hug his bearded face, and listen to his crazy stories. But I didn't want it to make my mom sad.

The sincerity of the letter was cut through with my dad's voice—silly and sarcastic and totally unlike the pious positivity that had been surrounding me in Fairfield. It felt like a distant strain of familiar music. He included a newspaper clipping of a poem he'd just published. Mom stared at it and then passed it over. She let us read it for ourselves.

NINJA FRUIT

My son sleeps toward the east
In his mood pajamas he dreams
And loves small animals to death
In the morning he wanders
Through the orchard
Picking apples
And at night, in his room
Stuffs broken glass
Into the fruit
And hides it near my picture,
Hoping I'll come back.

Stacey's face was blank while we read. Afterward, he said he wanted to go to his room. I wished that Dad had written a poem about me, although not that poem. That poem felt like a curse. Did he think he had broken us?

Dad's letter was followed by phone calls—he'd call in the evenings after Mom had come home from the dome. They'd have a hushed, brief conversation before she passed the phone to us.

I watched her talk to him intently. I didn't want him to make her cry but I also didn't want her to push him away, to scare him off and think we were so sad. When I got on the phone, I'd drag it to a small corner next to the couch and I'd cook up funny stories to tell him about school and my friends. I loved to hear him laugh—his voice on the phone was soft and thoughtful—and it egged me on to try to think of ways in which the earnest world I was living in could be made amusing. He teased me that I spoke so quietly perhaps I had become a spy, already practiced in whispering state secrets. He started speaking to me in a squeaky cartoon voice, pretending to be a guy named Bert, who was on an incredible cross-country journey to come see me and who wanted to be my best friend and was worried about my life there. I whispered my sarcastic stories back to him, snickering. But I didn't want Mom to hear me making jokes about our life—it felt like a betrayal.

Dad was also starting to send money even if it was only a fraction of the child support he had been ordered to pay when their divorce was finalized years earlier. Still, it made a difference. Now we could buy name-brand cereal, tickets for the movies on weekends, and new shoes. I started to imagine what life would be like if my dad lived in Fairfield. Would he come to school assemblies? Would he buy me designer jeans? Would he and Mom get remarried?

My mom had been dating a guy named Tim who was a tall, thin, computer programmer. He had big, geeky glasses and wisps of blond-ish hair that barely covered his balding head, and he was perpetually dressed for the dome in soft, loose clothing that hung off his bony frame. He was at least five years younger than Mom. They'd been set up by our next-door neighbors, an elegant and theatrical Canadian couple who were obsessed with ballroom dancing. They'd encouraged my mom to join evening classes with them and, as luck would have it, Tim was the only other person in the class who didn't have a partner. After they started dating, Tim and my mother would waltz around the small kitchen of our trailer, laughing as they bumped into the furniture. Their geeky romance made me squirm but there was hardly any way to escape it in our close quarters.

I liked the insecurity I saw on Tim's face as he watched my dad's reemergence with a weakling's suspicion. He never said anything, but he would look sad and detached when Stacey or I acted giddy or joyous after one of my dad's phone calls. We never exhibited any sign of pleasure around Tim in the hopes that this would expedite his departure.

He and my mom joined a self-help support group to allow them both to build confidence and take control of their lives. Or something. SET—Self-Empowerment Training—held seminars and weekly evening workshops that encouraged members to focus on their "wins" and be goal oriented. Started by a local therapist who also practiced TM, the curriculum seemed to go hand in hand with Maharishi's 200 percent mantra.

While Maharishi's administration certainly encouraged and profited from material success, there wasn't a lot of Vedic guidance on the subject. Maharishi seemed to think that all Americans were wealthy and that they should pay extra for things in order to appreciate them—that was his rationale for the high cost of his school, and the dome, and his Ayurvedic treatments. Now, SET was just one of many aim-for-success workshops that were burgeoning around towns as meditators like my mom became more focused on the brass tacks of getting ahead and being able to afford Maharishi's program.

Mom was always listening to tapes in the car from a shrieking, eccentric preacher from New York named Reverend Ike, who exhorted us to treat money like a lady and make her feel loved, romanced, and welcomed. She told us she would buy a gold Toyota Forerunner when her astrological fate changed direction and that she wouldn't have to work all the time and we could go on vacations out of Iowa and do all sorts of Ayurvedic treatments.

I also hoped that maybe if Dad came back, it would mean we wouldn't be so broke all the time. It felt like the whirlwind of Vedic living that Maharishi was increasingly advocating had priced us out of the Program and to the edges of the Movement. We couldn't afford the Amrit Kalash supplement that was supposed to be like the nectar of the gods. Mom said Maharishi promised the supplement would make you fly even higher at the dome and accelerate your evolution. And it was supposed to make kids smarter and healthier.

When we got sick and went to the Ayurvedic clinic, we would get a long list of Maharishi Ayurveda herbs to take and a look of panic would cross my mom's face. We couldn't afford the many prescribed supplements and spices that were meant to bring us in tune with Natural Law. I wanted all of that because it would make Mom happy, but the truth is, I wanted a bike without training wheels even more. I wanted posters for my walls and new sneakers. I imagined all the gifts that Dad might get me in California— things that would signal that my life was bigger than just another scholarship kid at the Maharishi School.

A few months later, Dad—aka Bert—decided to make good on his promises to come see us. He told us he was going to leave his life in San Francisco—including his sponsor and his network of AA friends—and come live in Fairfield. When we told Mom about this plan, her face got tight and sad but she didn't protest. She grew silent when Stacey and I talked about where we would take my dad when he got to town. The new Walmart? The domes? The gazebo in the town square? When I told my friends at school that my dad was moving to town, one girl gave me a funny look and asked: "Isn't he dead?" "No," I said, rolling my eyes, renouncing my years-long story. "He lives in California." I was so excited to move on to a new chapter.

My dad came back into our lives at what seemed like just the right moment. I was feeling marginalized in a binary world of townies versus gurus, meditators versus Americans, us versus them. I didn't like my mom's boyfriend or her newfound interest in cheesy financial self-help, or the Movement's emphasis on wealth as a sign of spiritual success. I didn't like being poor. I wanted to be defined in ways that no one here would understand—and a mysterious father showing up from California was the perfect solution to my identity quest.

Dad's world seemed cosmopolitan and cool—a whole other reality. He was cynical and he loved making art, drinking coffee, and smoking cigarettes. He read the *New Yorker* and the *Paris Review* and came up with wild, strange, funny stories all the time. His disruptive, contrarian voice was a welcome one.

Dad's return to our life if only by phone also seemed to have a powerful effect on my brother, who was fast becoming a star student. That spring, he had received the coveted Maharishi School of the Age of Enlightenment "Ideal Student" award for his class, for his good grades and for embodying Maharishi's principles of the Science of Creative Intelligence. Stacey had always been a good student but school didn't always hold his interest. When we lived in New York, Mom had his IQ tested and she insinuated—never giving a number—that Stacey's was very high. ("Yours too," she said, as an afterthought.) But now he spent hours in Courtenay's basement working on his end-of-the-year science fair project with her husband, a scientist.

I was jealous. Lately I'd lose myself for long stretches in school, staring out the window, not quite able to tune in to the drone of Vedic Knowledge streaming forth from my teacher. We seemed to be doing less and less actual work—like reading and math—and spending more and more time just talking in the classroom about Maharishi's Knowledge. The notes on my report cards never seemed to inspire the enthusiasm that Stacey's did. I seemed to be underachieving in a way that I didn't understand.

"Orderliness doesn't dampen creativity but enhances it!" read one report card. "Maharishi says 'Enjoy greater efficiency and accomplish more.'" Cloaked in forward-looking positivity, this was criticism Maharishi School style. The subtext was clear: I was not ideal.

While our financial situation was becoming increasingly perilous in Iowa, on the other side of the planet, Maharishi was having money challenges of his own. Over the last decade, he'd continued to purchase properties in the United States and Europe. He had hundreds of nonprofit organizations throughout the world, and the understanding in Fairfield was that most of those earnings were sent back to what everyone called, "International," Maharishi's Global Headquarters. By 1988, the Maharishi's conspicuous acquisitions prompted Indian tax authorities to raid his sprawling complex in Delhi, which made headlines across India. Maharishi moved his operations from Switzerland to the sleepy town of Vlodrop, Holland, where he had purchased a former monastery.

Perhaps more humiliating for Maharishi was the fallout from what should have been one of his crowning glories. In 1991, an article appeared in the *Journal of the American Medical Association* touting the virtues of Transcendental Meditation and his recently launched Maharishi Ayurveda. The article used several scientific studies to support the claim that Maharishi's Ayurvedic herbal products were effective in treating a host of ailments. Deepak Chopra, whom Maharishi had been grooming as a leader of his Movement, was one of the lead authors. Until 1988, Chopra had been president of the sole Ayurveda distribution company, and he remained a board member in 1991, meaning that he had a financial interest in the research. The article was quickly savaged by critics who cried foul that the authors had a vested interest in the products being touted. JAMA issued a rebuttal later that year, and then Chopra filed a libel suit against JAMA and others. The suit was later dismissed.

There had been a tangible shift in Maharishi and the Movement around this time, from mantras to products. Maharishi trademarked dozens of items with his name (Maharishi Honey, Maharishi Veda Vision), and services and technologies seemed to have mushroomed at this point as well. In Fairfield, his branded items—such as special spices and teas—were considered fundamental to the Program and, therefore, always sold well. Around this time, the annual cost of tuition for the elementary school also shot up from a maximum of $1,950 to as much as $3,000. I had the sense from my teachers and the administrators that I was supposed to be more thankful for being at the school on a scholarship. When I rolled my eyes in class, or pushed back at my teachers, asking for, say, evidence that the Age of Enlightenment was dawning, I'd often get a sharp rebuke or an exhausted sigh. There were a few times when I was darkly reminded that "we all had to work extra hard to fund-raise and support Maharishi's vision for the school, so that our scholarship students could stay with us." The cost of attending the dome jumped from $30 a month to $100.

On the day my father arrived, Mom arranged for a babysitter and said she would be doing a long program at the dome. I sat in my bedroom, ignoring my homework, staring out the window. My stomach felt queasy. I could see the sun sinking behind the orange horizon line of the trailer park. From this vantage point, I could see the cars as they came down the street. We lived on Chroman Drive—named after one of Maharishi's wealthy benefactors—which was one-way, and although maybe only five hundred yards long, it had four stop signs and three speed bumps. Something about all that meditation inspired people to drive very slowly and cautiously. Dad had called from a pay phone a few hours earlier, saying he was about two hundred miles away and making his way across western Iowa toward us.

I threw myself on my bed. I couldn't quite think straight and I certainly couldn't read the teen romance in my hand.

I could hear Stacey in the bedroom next to me, plucking away on his new electric guitar. We both couldn't wait, but Stacey didn't want to share those feelings with me—he scoffed when I bounced up and down after Dad had said on the phone that he was so close to our house.

I tried to keep in check the crazy hope I was feeling. Mom had warned me, her mouth taut and careful, that Dad might not be the way we remembered. She reminded me that he was an alcoholic and to not expect too much from him.

When I heard the hollow knocking sound on the metal trailer door, I almost jumped out of my skin. How had I missed his car pulling up outside? As I leaped to my feet, I heard the babysitter open the door and murmur something. I walked past Stacey's room where he was getting up slowly, avoiding my eyes. He tossed his guitar to the side, and walked behind me as I ran-walked to the back door.

There he was—handsome face, soft scruffy beard, a halo of shaggy honey brown hair, crisp white button-down shirt, black jeans, white sneakers. He swiftly pulled Stacey and me into him in an almost frantic hug. I felt Stacey next to me, holding on to Dad's waist a little stiffly.

I tried making myself smaller to nuzzle against my father's stomach. I inhaled the smell of his cigarettes and peppermint Life Savers. I felt his beard brush against the top of my head. For a moment, we didn't say anything, the three of us pressed together. Dad started to cry; I felt his tears falling onto my arms. He let out a wild, snarling sob. It was the saddest sound I'd ever heard—loud and guilty and full of pain, as if he was waking up from some terrible dream and discovering himself here with us, suddenly grown into awkward adolescents. He seemed to choke on his tears, and I tried to nuzzle deeper into him to comfort him. To remind him that I was the same little kid who loved to be tossed into the air and watch his wide hands turn into deranged puppets.

But Dad stood up and backed away, and as he wiped away his tears, he abruptly looked at us for a moment as if he were watching a movie of the past instead of being in here with us in the little hallway of our trailer. I flinched as I watched him retreat from us—his eyes turning inward. Then, just as quickly, he snapped back into focus. In the funny squeaky voice of Bert, he said, "Finally, I'm here. I couldn't stand to be with Fred any longer."

Ignoring our sitter—who was sitting at the kitchen table reading her mystery and pretending not to notice our reunion—we dragged Dad to our bedrooms to show him our stuff. He'd brought Stacey a bunch of music tapes, but for me he had brought a very old copy of *The Wizard of Oz*. He looked at me meaningfully. "I think you'll really treasure this," he said. "Dorothy was from Kansas, you're from Iowa." I fingered the old thick pages and thought for a moment how, like Maharishi, the wizard was powerful and never seen.

Sitting on the bed, we examined our gifts. Whenever one of us got quiet, Dad would start talking like Bert—"Please tell Fred to stop smoking!"—and wipe his wet face with his hands.

Dad found an apartment on the other side of town from the campus. For a moment, I felt the unfamiliar popularity of having two parents live in the same town. Within a few weeks, though, he told us he had to leave; he said he couldn't sleep in Fairfield because it was too quiet. He told Mom he didn't like feeling like everyone in town knew that he had abandoned his family for so long. He told us that he didn't like how all the people from the TM Movement made him feel like an outcast. He joked that they acted like Maharishi robots. We nodded like we understood, but I didn't. Soon, he moved to Iowa City—about an hour from Fairfield by car—where he still had friends from when he'd gone to graduate school there.

After a few weeks, Dad started doing a local comedy cable-access show with his friend Dan Coffey, who had been in his graduate program at the Writers Workshop a decade earlier. Like Dad, Dan was sober and offbeat—he'd been in a comedy troupe called Duck's Breath that had toured nationally. But unlike Dad, he was a hugely loud exhibitionist who reveled in embarrassing people. They were a perfect match.

Dan played an over-the-top character called Dr. Science, a mad, ranting scientist who was always screwing up. My dad played the straight man, quietly muttering nihilistic critiques of his friend and the world. They called their show *Koralville Konfidential*, named for a bland suburb adjacent to Iowa City. I liked to watch the show though I never really understood it. I liked how my dad looked on television, handsome and quiet, taking little barbed shots at his friend. Usually it was just the two of them in a studio, sitting on chairs, sounding off about absolutely nothing. The idea of doing something like this—a nonaspirational, non-revenue-producing creative project was eye opening. I loved the idea of doing something just because you'd thought of it, instead of doing something to get Enlightenment, say, or World Peace.

Dad would talk to us for the long stretches of rural roads on our drives between Iowa City and Fairfield—about how screwed up his parents were, how odd the women he was dating were, and the crazy drunken episodes that he and his friends had gotten into when they were teenagers. I liked the stories about him being wild—they were exciting and made him seem like he was this really entertaining character in a funny movie. But I didn't really like hearing about the girlfriends. I'd had my fill of the guys Mom dated, and I didn't want to become the confidante for my dad as well.

Dad's apartment sat above a law office in an old Victorian house near the University of Iowa. It reeked of the coffee he constantly brewed and the cigarettes he smoked while hanging out the window.

It was filled with the papier-mâché sculptures of macabre angels and tilted skyscrapers that he had started to make in his spare time.

After several hushed conversations on the porch outside our trailer, Mom agreed to let us start spending every other weekend with our dad. Mom was hardly ever home these days anyway. She and Tim were spending three nights a week at meetings that they called "processing"—an outgrowth of SET where they would repeat affirmations and pledges of encouragement for each other. She rarely allowed us to talk about Dad with her. When we imitated his jokes or parroted his sarcasm, she would immediately snap at us.

Our visits to Iowa City were everything that Fairfield was not. Dad let us eat hamburgers and ice cream and we got to stay up late and watch *Saturday Night Live*. We felt suddenly connected to a faraway urban world that was sophisticated and cool. I would roll around on his futon bed, laughing hysterically at Deep Thoughts, and the Church Lady, and I quickly embraced the satirical lack of respect in the show, trying to fold it into my own awkward attempts at humor.

In the morning we'd wake up to Dad typing away on his typewriter, an ashtray full of cigarettes letting us know that he'd been up for hours. Dad pored over the newspaper and made jokes about world events. He spent all his free time—and his frenetic nondrinking energy—on making his elaborate sculptures and writing poetry.

It also felt like he engaged us as intellectual equals—asking us questions about whether or not we believed in God, and what we thought of Maharishi. He told us he was agnostic, which meant you believed that the origin of the universe and what powered it was unknowable. The idea that you could define yourself by the decision not to have an answer was so new to me. Immediately, I was an agnostic too.

Dad also quizzed us about the Maharishi School and the things we did there. When I told him that our meditations were now graded in school—and that I kept being marked down for opening my eyes—he laughed and teased us, saying that we were living in a cult. I knew the word but thought it had to do with crazy people who took drugs and wore weird clothes and killed themselves. Dad said that we had to be careful not to believe everything Maharishi said and that our teachers didn't know all the answers. He would mutter asides about Maharishi, about him wanting to make a lot of money and be powerful, or about my teachers being uptight weirdos who couldn't think for themselves. I laughed because I wanted Dad to see that I understood, but it didn't quite make sense to me. Not yet.

CHAPTER ELEVEN

Your Meditation
Brought Down the Great Wall

"Jai Guru Dev," Mrs. Hall, my sixth-grade teacher, said softly. "Let's slowly open our eyes." I blinked, feeling, as usual, sleepy and listless. Due to overcrowding in the lower school, our classroom had moved across the street from the main school to a corner of the dining hall. Though enrollment in the Maharishi School had been booming lately—the ceaseless fund-raising was at full tilt—the reality for us was not gleaming new facilities but rather the mildewed old dormitory building left over from the Parsons College days.

I could smell the curried scents of lunch being prepared. Mrs. Hall fiddled with the intercom on her desk as she tuned in to hear our school principal, Mr. Balf, read our morning announcements. "Jai Guru Dev," he said, his voice crackling over the intercom. Mr. Balf had white hair and reminded me of George Washington—a man he liked to quote almost as much as he liked to quote Maharishi.

Mr. Balf took the announcements very seriously, giving a mini lecture each day on Being and Consciousness. He began, as always, with a quote from Maharishi. "The formula for producing maximum results is to disregard the obstacles and negative influences which offer resistance to the performance of action. The doer should engage in action and continue until the desired results are achieved," he read, his voice crackling over the intercom and growing louder with each sentence. "When the standard of consciousness is raised through the process of meditation, the action performed at that higher level of life and energy and intelligence will have an overriding influence on karma from the past and will produce maximum results."

I fidgeted in my seat. Lately, it felt like most of Maharishi's teachings for us were about leadership and accomplishment. I heard less and less about transcending and more about succeeding—both at home and at school.

We'd also recently had a steady stream of guests—people from the outside world who were very interested in our education. Practically every week, it seemed, some visiting dignitary would peer into the classroom to watch us meditate or sing Maharishi's songs: the guy who founded Walmart; Joe Namath; one of the Beach Boys. They would stand attentively at the back of the class as we talked about Native American tribes and how their shared histories were a perfect example of Maharishi's principle that Harmony Exists in Diversity. Could it be that what we were talking about *was* really smart and complicated despite my doubts?

Mrs. Hall had also begun to spend some time each day teaching us what it meant to be a leader. She would cite different historical figures—Abraham Lincoln, Eleanor Roosevelt—and then explain how their successes showed that they had lived according to Maharishi's principles. They hadn't practiced TM but their essential connection to the Unified Field—I gathered because of their brilliance—meant that Nature had supported their efforts.

At the conclusion of the announcements, Mr. Balf paused in midsentence. We could hear him whispering to someone. "All grades should head directly over to the campus theater for an all-school assembly," he said sharply. "Now."

It was November 10, 1989. We filed into the campus assembly hall one by one. The room reverberated with shouting and laughter. I looked around to see if I could find Stacey or any of his friends—it was so exciting to be around all the older kids, despite the fact that they strode past me without even looking down. I was in sixth grade, which meant that to exactly half the school I was completely invisible.

Dr. Bevan Morris walked onstage, his chubby body stuffed into a yellow silk suit, his pink tie matching the color of his cherubic cheeks.

As the one most trusted by Maharishi, Bevan delivered all of the guru's important messages. He sat down heavily in the gold upholstered chair placed at the center of the empty stage. He closed his eyes, as if in reverence to something we hadn't yet noticed. Whispering curiously among ourselves, our teachers shushed us sternly.

Slowly, Dr. Morris whispered into a microphone that had been placed in front of him: "Jai Guru Dev." A long pause followed. Tears began to roll down his waxen face.

He opened his eyes halfway, his lashes fluttering. He started to giggle in an awkward imitation of Maharishi's impish laugh. "Children. I have something so beautiful to tell you," he announced. "The Dawn of the Age of Enlightenment is here! World Peace is on its way!"

He had everyone's attention. "As Maharishi has predicted, we are in a golden age of Ved. It is because of you—each and every one of you and your daily practice of meditation—that World Peace has come. It is here! This week the wall in Berlin was torn down. It is an incredible moment for humankind and a sign that the Dawn of the Age of Enlightenment is here and it is all thanks to you students, the shining light of peace and Maharishi's wisdom. We have toppled the wall with our meditation!"

I shifted in the itchy auditorium seat and looked at my scuffed brown loafers. Inside my shoe, I wiggled my toe in the hole of my worn white tights. I felt an unfamiliar cutting sensation in my stomach. I looked over at my friend Orpita but she was beaming up at Bevan like everyone else. Some girls from my class hugged each other and let out little cheers. Teachers gasped and laughed. This was the news we had all been waiting for—but I felt strangely outside it all.

My meditations hadn't been any more powerful than usual. There were times when my mantra could take me to a remote and still space inside myself—the world dropped away and I was left with nothing but a warm sense of aliveness. But more often, I told my mom I was meditating when instead I hid under my bedcovers eating sour cherry candy balls and reading my Sweet Valley High books. I knew what Dr. Morris said couldn't be right. There was no way that my meditations were responsible for monumental change on the other side of the world. I imagined what my dad would say about all of us applauding ourselves for toppling the Soviet empire. I knew he would laugh out loud but with a tone far more judgmental than the gentle jokes he usually made about the TM world. I suddenly felt like I was in *Invasion of the Body Snatchers* and everyone around me was a stranger.

In October 1989, Maharishi had arranged for a second massive conference to demonstrate the Maharishi Effect. The Taste of Heaven on Earth Assembly in Fairfield took place the first two weeks of the month. It was the Taste of Utopia all over again, with an influx of four thousand people who gathered for two weeks to meditate and delve into Maharishi's Knowledge.

This time, Mom was too broke to do the course—and she didn't have a secret donor to pay her way. Our financial situation was a bigger issue than ever. The mysterious donor who had initially paid for us had long since disappeared. That summer, Mom had told Stacey she could only afford to send one of us to the Maharishi School and since he was older, it made more sense for him to switch schools. I overheard this conversation but I didn't say much. I was deathly afraid of going to public school and noted the stony anger with which Stacey greeted the news. I remembered the kids throwing rocks at him at Lincoln and shuddered.

At public school, Stacey's grades started to slip. His perfect grades quickly became Cs and Ds. His teachers from school would call and tell my mom that he refused to even hand in homework. When Mom was at the dome, he would shove me out of the way wordlessly, his disgust for me an almost physical presence in the room. I felt young and coddled and contemptible as I watched him suffer. I knew how cruel the townies could be. Even when we spent the weekends with my father, Stacey seemed surly and quiet. My father didn't take Stacey's gloominess well. He seemed to go out of his way to yell at him when my mom was around in a naked attempt to win her approval. But even when she wasn't around, Dad was hard on Stacey for the slightest infraction, lashing out at him for the smallest sign of disrespect.

Stacey had grown his dirty blond hair out, with long bangs that hung over his eyes. He was a fanatical skater, and spent long hours in the abandoned industrial part of town, skating with older kids.

He covered his walls with pages from skateboard magazines. He'd lock himself inside his room, playing the guitar or blasting the Violent Femmes. His disdain for my mom, my dad, the Movement, and me vibrated from him. For so long, my brother had been the person I understood the best in the world. When he would tire of his teasing and relent to play with me, we could spend hours together laughing and creating imaginary worlds together, intricate and hilarious. He had my father's imagination, coupled with my mother's sweetness. But now he talked to Mom as if each word cost him dearly, biting out each one as he spoke. It left no space for me to be outwardly anything but cooperative and respectful.

Mom and Tim broke up without much fanfare. The bad news was that when my mom didn't have a boyfriend, it felt like a steady stream of suitors began vying for her attention. Male friends seemed to be always dropping by for a homemade dinner or eagerly driving her to one of her evening support groups. I saw all of them as inferior beings competing with me for time with my mom.

But just when I thought the long line might go on forever, Rick started showing up every night. I could see that Rick was meant to be handsome—there was a chiseled quality about his face—but mostly he looked sinister. He always seemed to be plotting something and never bothered to talk to Stacey or me. Instead of passively ignoring my little cruelties—as my mother's boyfriends in the past often did—he would erupt, taking my mom aside and complaining about my behavioral problems by using language that made me sound like an outsider. "Liz, your daughter likely doesn't appreciate the rice and dal you make for her every night." For that, he earned a merciless silence from me.

With Mom, however, he was frequently animated and chivalrous; he was always helping her carry things, bringing her flowers.

In an instant, however, his mood would change. Despite his tough looks and attitude, he would often have sulky, childlike tantrums, insisting that my mom join him in her bedroom for long talks. He was diabetic, which meant he would sometimes feel faint and float off to my mom's room to lie down. He always seemed vulnerable and needy.

Rick drove a golden sports car that he kept in impeccable condition. He loved the Grateful Dead and flaunted his fandom— dancing bears on the bumper, a concert tape always in the cassette player, stories about all the concerts he had attended. He lived in Utopia Park but on the other side from us. He had recently gotten divorced from another woman, who also had two kids.

One day at school the older kid took me aside and said he'd heard that Rick and my mom were going to get married. It was the first I'd heard of it.

"Just watch out," the kid told me. "Mom says he used to hit his first wife."

I went home that night feeling like I had a death sentence. I had never liked Rick, but now the idea that he was some sort of mom abuser really put me over the edge. I actively started plotting ways to sabotage their relationship. And what was this marriage talk?

Sure enough, weeks later, I was rummaging around in my mom's bathroom, where she kept a little wooden cabinet filled with dangly earrings as well as feathers, beads, and little wooden creatures. I noticed a long gleaming silver necklace made of hundreds of interlocking slender circles. It looked like something a knight would wear. I picked it up; it was heavy, like a thick collar for a wild animal. In my hands it felt ominous. I sensed it was a sign of something bad to come. I carried it into my mom's room where she was doing her asanas, her legs raised above her head in plow position.

"What is this?" I asked.

Immediately, my mom rolled back onto the ground. Her face turned red. She stood up and took the necklace from my hands.

"I was going to talk to you later about this, with your brother," she said, sounding huffy and a little bit resigned. "Rick asked me to marry him."

"So does that mean you are getting married?"

"I guess so," she said. Which struck me as a weird response.

"Did he get you a ring?" I asked.

"No, he got me that necklace. You know, I don't really like rings."

"Do you like the necklace?" I asked.

"No," she said, and laughed, looking me straight in the eye. She gave me a big hug. "Don't worry about it, baby." There was still hope, I thought.

The next morning a funny old Indian lady in a sari showed up at the trailer door. Mom and Rick ushered her in and began whispering to her in hushed tones. I was flung out on the living room couch reading a book—or at least pretending to as I eyed them suspiciously.

"I'd like you guys to come join us for a puja," my mom said, suddenly looming over me. Stacey—who had been sitting in an armchair strumming his guitar—marched past us into his bedroom and slammed the door. I felt sick. I had hoped that my mom's vagueness about the engagement meant it wasn't real, that maybe Rick had just had one of his dramatic fits and given her the necklace and soon it would all be forgotten.

But a puja? This was a traditional Indian ceremony conducted to celebrate major life moments. It was one step away from a wedding ceremony. I reluctantly trudged after them to my mom's bedroom where the Indian lady sat kneeling in her sari in front of a painted photograph of Guru Dev that usually rested on top of my mom's dresser between baby photos of me and Stacey. My mom and Rick kneeled behind the lady. She lit some incense and began chanting. The room filled with a heavy smoke and a camphor smell. I quietly sat cross-legged behind them, still feeling uneasy.

There was not a firm date set for the wedding, but Rick and his moods seemed to increasingly monopolize my mom. Both Stacey and I retreated into the back of the trailer to our bedrooms, where we lived in quiet worlds of our own making.

At fourteen, Stacey was a handsome kid. His looks combined my parents' best features—blazing blue eyes, long eyelashes, delicate bone structure. But he didn't pursue girls the way his friends did. Watching the line of schmucks outside my mom's door had turned him off to hitting on women. He kept mostly to himself, earphones on, blasting Led Zeppelin.

But that fall he started hanging out with a friend who was completely off the Program. Matt was seventeen years old and had just moved from Alaska—where he had dropped out of high school—to live with his dad in Utopia Park. Matt had a heart-shaped face and long scraggly blond hair and the kind of easy natural coolness that served as pheromones for teenagers—everyone seemed attracted to his diffident sweetness. He and Stacey would spend long hours in Stacey's tiny room, picking at the guitar and reading *The Anarchist Cookbook*. While Mom was at the Dome, they would boil banana peels to try to make homemade bombs and smoke Mom's poppy seeds from the spice rack. I would hole up in my room—pointedly playing my Bob Dylan albums loud enough for Matt to hear so he would understand that I too was not interested in the sound of the Ved.

One evening, I said good night to my mom, who was sitting at the dinner table with her fiancé. It was past Stacey's nine o'clock curfew and she seemed anxious that he wasn't home yet. As I turned off my light and curled up under the covers, I heard the trailer door squeak open. And then I heard the murmur of voices. I tiptoed out of bed, opened my door, and peered down the hall. Stacey was standing in the doorway with both my mom and Rick blocking his entrance. His voice sounded loose and sort of silly to me.

"Are you drunk?" Mom shrieked at him. I could tell, even though I couldn't see her face, that she was crying.

"Naw, Mom, let me go to bed, I'm fine," Stacey said, trying to push past Rick. From out of nowhere, Rick threw Stacey's body against the wall, pinning his shoulders. I cowered in the shadows.

"Don't speak to your mother like that, asshole!" Rick shouted.

"You're drunk, you're drunk," my mother kept saying, as if Stacey had murdered someone and was covered with blood.

But Stacey was whimpering now too, scared by Rick's violent turn. "No, no. Just let me go to bed."

Mom turned and saw me standing in the doorway. "I'm taking Stacey to the hospital," she said. I didn't say anything. Rick police-walked Stacey out the door, his hands firmly on his shoulders. I heard the car doors slam and they were gone.

The next morning, I waited for as long as I could before I wandered out to the kitchen. Both Stacey's and Mom's doors were shut. I poured myself a bowl of cereal and sat at the dining room table, staring out at the street. The trees were mostly without leaves, the sky bleached an autumnal gray. After a while, Mom emerged, and I could tell that she had been meditating as she padded quietly out to the kitchen and motioned for me to come into her bedroom.

"Stacey is grounded for a year," she announced. I stared at her. I didn't look forward to a year of Stacey trapped at home with nothing to do but terrorize me. "Claire, he came home drunk. You need to understand how serious this is. Your father is an alcoholic, which means both of you stand a good chance of becoming alcoholics yourselves."

Perhaps she sensed me questioning her in my silence so she changed tactics. "Do you remember Marsten Green?" she asked. Marsten was a kid a few years older than Stacey. When we first moved to Fairfield, Marsten and his family had lived on our block. One of my mom's many jobs had included helping Marsten's mom in her catering business, making vats of vegetarian lasagna and baked tofu for local events.

"He's dead," she said, her voice quivering. "They found him last week in a cornfield, dead." Mom proceeded to tell me the horror story—Marsten had taken some huge amount of LSD and wandered off through a field of towering corn in the middle of a hot summer day. He'd become disoriented or dehydrated or maybe had a heart attack. He'd been missing for months until a local farmer had plowed his field and found a skeleton and the remaining shreds of a Metallica T-shirt, along with strands of Marsten's long, dark hair.

For as long as I could remember, Mom's bedside table had been piled with books on dependence, alcoholism, and addiction. Mom had raised Stacey and me with the understanding that we had some sort of genetic tendency toward addiction—as if there were a time bomb inside us. I'd mostly tried to block this idea out, mutely chalking it up to more self-empowerment speak. Inside, though, I defiantly assured myself that our family demons would not haunt me. Or Stacey. But the image of this teenage kid I'd known dying alone in a cornfield was horrifying and immediate. To make matters worse, my mom told me if Stacey continued to drink and smoke pot, he could end up like Marsten. From that moment on I began to live in fear that my brother would die alone, on drugs.

Mom's response to her fears was to seek further refuge in Maharishi's Knowledge. It had been recently announced on campus that Maharishi was restoring the ancient practice of Vedic astrology, Maharishi Jyotish. A recent five-page story in the TM-affiliated local paper *The Source* described it this way: "For more than 30 years, Maharishi has taught that transcending is the basis for gaining higher knowledge and progress in life. He now feels that the time has come to build the mansion of all-knowingness on the foundation of pure consciousness." Maharishi Jyotish could be learned—for a fee—by those who practiced the TM-Siddhi technique. In moving beyond TM, they would, as the Maharishi promised, "rewrite destiny."

Maharishi Jyotish wasn't only about getting your chart read—part of the rewriting of destiny was the use of Maharishi Jyotish gem stones, which were now on sale at a local jeweler. These specially cut gems were supposedly connected with each of the planets. By wearing them, one would be even more fully aligned with nature.

Mom managed to scrape together the money to get Stacey's jyotish chart done. Perhaps she felt she could change the dark future she foresaw for him. I was immediately indignant and jealous when I was told that there wasn't enough money to do mine. This meant that Stacey would know his prospects—how much money he would make and when he was going to die—while I would be left to the winds of fate. Some guy down the block in Utopia Park supplemented his fourth-grade teacher's salary by doing these charts. One evening after the Program, my mom and Stacey went to his trailer for the reading, leaving me to pace and seethe in ours.

An hour later, Stacey swung open the front door, walked to his room, and slammed the door. Mom placed a little pile of papers on the table and went to the sink to make a cup of tea. I went to the kitchen table and picked up the papers, which showed a geometric web laid out with a list of numbers and dates.

"It's probably better that you don't look at that, Claire," she said, snatching the papers from me. "That belongs to Stacey."

"What did it say?" I asked.

She looked at me with a grave face. "Stacey is in Rahu. We both are. This is the most difficult period there is and it lasts sometimes for twenty years. It means everything will be hard for us, everything will be challenging."

I'd been hearing about Rahu for months now—ever since my mom had her jyotish chart done and discovered she was in this inauspicious phase of her life. She wasn't alone—a lot of grown-ups talked about the challenges of being in Rahu over tofu dogs at backyard barbecues. There seemed to be a certain pride in being in Rahu, like you were a real bad ass—enduring the onslaught of an angry god. Also, you were exempt from ever trying to make things work out since you were doomed anyway.

In Vedic astrology, Rahu is not an actual planet but more like a dark energy vortex. (Apparently they had thought there was a planet there, but later discovered they were wrong.) Rahu's energy wasn't good. The god Rahu was depicted as a severed serpent head riding in a chariot drawn by eight black horses. Solar eclipses occurred, it was believed, when Rahu swallowed the sun. He challenged your karma, forcing tough choices, but he could also cast lives into chaos and mystery and misfortune.

I began to feel his shadowy presence in our home. I wasn't quite sure what to make of Mom and Stacey's new shared affiliation with this shadowy planet monster. Something about it made me feel a little separate from them—much was now being attributed to Rahu and perhaps I felt left out because, as far as I knew, I was not cursed. But there was also a quiet voice inside me whispering that there was no way planets were deciding the course of our lives.

CHAPTER TWELVE

The Costs of Karma

Everything changed for me. I felt like I had been thrust out of the circus tent, ever since the fall of the Berlin Wall, and was now outside peering back in at the ridiculousness and chaos. I felt at a strange remove as all the adults around me—my mom, my neighbors, my teachers—unquestioningly built their lives around the Program. Even the way they spoke about it: "The Program," or "Maharishi's Knowledge," or Enlightenment—why did everything that came out of Maharishi's mouth become capitalized and important? As a kid on scholarship, I had the sense from my teachers and the administrators that I was supposed to be more thankful for being at the school. But I couldn't help myself—all of the talk in class of living according to Maharishi's vision was more than I could bear.

During this period, Stacey, who was still grounded, acted like an angry hostage. But we had one shared point of interest: movies. When Mom left for the Program in the evening, we worked together—usually without any verbal communication—jacking up the air-conditioning, making ourselves a forbidden non-Ayurvedic snack, and turning on a movie.

Fairfield's first video rental store had opened that summer, and it had been life changing. Adventureland Video, a long dark tunnel of a store, was packed from floor to ceiling with VHS movies. Often on Fridays Mom would take us to Adventureland and let us pick out a movie or two for the weekend, something to watch while she and Rick went to their weekly processing meeting. I didn't cry now when Mom left or sit next to the window and wait for her to return. I still missed her, but now I looked forward to her leaving so that I could disappear into movies and candy.

Stacey loved action movies, skating movies, and anything that involved karate, but I had become a classic movie buff. I diligently worked my way through the Marilyn Monroe titles, then James Dean and Grace Kelly and Cary Grant and Clark Gable. But what really excited me was the video store's large collection of Alfred Hitchcock films. My mom raised her eyebrows at my selection but somehow still let me take home *39 Steps* and *Strangers on a Train*. While I wasn't even allowed to watch PG-13 movies—or anything else that conjured up negativity or a lack of alignment with the Laws of Nature—the classic films passed as educational or historical.

I worked chronologically from a list that I had copied from a Hitchcock biography that I had checked out from the public library next door to Adventureland. I would use whatever small savings I had put together for the week—$1 from my grandmother in Florida and such—and buy a small bag of candy. Sitting in front of our little TV screen, watching these glamorous people drink cocktails and argue about infidelity and murder, was the ultimate escape from Utopia Park. These old movies became the identity cape that I used to cloak myself with at school—no one else shared my interest and I liked that. Whenever I wanted, I could enter my own secret world, full of dashing men in dark suits and buxom blondes with hidden agendas.

When Mrs. Hall announced that each of us would do a social studies project on a person of our choice who embodied one of Maharishi's principles of SCI, I decided I would do Marilyn Monroe. I had just finished two biographies of her and so I was deeply versed in her life, her travails and triumphs. It was a stretch, I knew, but I could relate anything at this point to Maharishi's principles. As each student took their turn saying which woman they'd chosen as the embodiment of the ideal—mostly mothers, teachers, and first ladies—I tingled with anticipation. When I announced I would be doing my project on Marilyn Monroe, my classmates stared and my teacher grimaced. A few minutes later she walked me out to the hall, her face contorted, as if she had just found out that *I* had been popping sleeping pills and sleeping with the president. Still, I insisted on doing it, assuring her that Marilyn perfectly embodied one of Maharishi's favorite Vedic truisms: *Do Less and Accomplish More.*

Lately, I'd been irked by the increasing emphasis by my teachers on embodying Maharishi's "feminine ideals." I'd always been taught that my brother and I were equals and resented this idea that girls were supposed to act differently.

"If one were to visit a traditional family in India, the home of the Veda, one would notice at once that the lady of the house is a graceful figure, radiating an almost palpable value of silence, and yet at the same time, she is very dynamic as she lays out course upon course of food for her guests and her family—attending to every detail for the comfort of all around her," read an article called "The Vedic Woman" I'd come across in *The Source.* "It would seem her whole life was one of servitude. But stay a little longer and watch—one will see becoming very evident one interesting fact: there will probably not be a single decision made in that household without consulting her. The entire family looks to her for ultimate wisdom—they have sensed that at the basis of her very existence is this wisdom that comes from knowing, from knowledge."

The article went on to celebrate the feminine virtues of a home-focused life of quiet acceptance with backseat control the only means of exerting power. That I might be expected to embody this retrograde role model irritated me, but, even more, I hated that my mom might feel belittled because she couldn't live up to this standard. For as long as I could remember, I'd watched her juggle jobs to support us entirely. And yet she kept a quote from Maharishi on the wall of her bedroom that exhorted women to be sweet, nurturing, and gentle.

The summer before I began seventh grade, I took on a new stance: at the party but not of the party. While my mom was at work, I would spend the entire day reading, trying to finish at least a book a day. Around lunchtime, I'd wander into the kitchen, avoiding Stacey and his wrath. I'd pull out some of the grilled tofu and rice to eat, all the while staying focused on my book.

Stacey and I kept our doors locked, relying on that thin partition of plywood and vinyl wood covering to hide our lives from each other. To Stacey, I was the lucky one. I never got in trouble, I never voiced dissent, and I got to go to private school.

Most summer afternoons, I'd walk through town, slowly kicking rocks along the broken sidewalks, in my own world. Sometimes I'd wander to a vacant lot with my friend Orpita—who also lived in Utopia Park—and we would try to smoke the cigarette butts we found or talk about what it would be like to drink alcohol.

Usually, I had to meet my mom at the town square by four o'clock. She had a new job working for a meditator who had started a company that sold cheerful, cartoonlike maps of tourist attractions in Iowa. Mom would laugh to herself while drawing little puffy clouds, serpentine roads, and fat farmers in overalls. She had a way of making everything look pudgy and adorable—even a squat little train station on a map of Dubuque. It was the first time she seemed really happy in a job.

If I arrived early, I would go to the library to check out books on joke telling and astrology—in preparation for a future life I imagined for myself, where I lived in New York, went to glamorous parties, and worked as a high-powered lawyer. (The jokes were to charm my new friends and the astrology to predict their futures!) Sometimes I'd go to a department store called Spurgeon's underneath the offices of Mapmakers. The lights were always flickering in there, and half of them were usually shut off. Spurgeon's looked like they hadn't placed a new order in years, with most of the clothes tagged with a hot pink or green sale sticker. The polyester clothing and preppy knitwear didn't appeal to the wealthy meditators who favored soft pastel linens and silks imported from India—it was no surprise that the store was on its last legs. My interest was the candy counter downstairs. I would scrape together a bit of change from around the house to buy a little white paper sack filled with sour cherry balls or gummy watermelon slices. I'd pop one in my mouth and suck on it, pulling all the artificial sweetness out as quickly as possible and then chomp away on its plastic jellyness. If there was an opposite taste to the Ayurvedic Rasayanas and chutneys and spices I was supposed to eat, this was it.

By August that summer, my mom had become even more preoccupied with our finances. She would spend evenings at her drafting table in the living room with little pieces of checkered paper, trying to move numbers around in a way that would make them work. She was only working part-time at Mapmakers so that she could spend most weekday mornings volunteering at the Maharishi School kindergarten in order to pay for my tuition.

My dad was paying child support from his job as a waiter at the Iowa River Power restaurant—the only fancy restaurant in Iowa City. He would pack together his tips in an envelope and hand them over to my mom every month. But it wasn't even close to enough to pay for my tuition. That job also meant that he had to work on the weekends, so we saw him less.

Meanwhile, the meditators were still generating an economic boom in Fairfield. Retail sales for the city went up 227 percent from 1976 to 1988. The county's assessed property value around that same time grew tenfold. Between 1980 and 1984, personal income rose 55 percent for the city. There were reports that in the town of nine thousand people, there were twenty-two millionaires. All of this was seen as evidence of the Super Radiance Effect—the meditation and flying technique were transforming this unlikely corner of Iowa and it was Maharishi's Knowledge that deserved the credit. From his base in India, Maharishi continued to call on us to use our meditation to create prosperity and funnel that back to his various projects.

Whether it was the rising cost of the dome, the school tuition, or the deluge of Maharishi Vedic products for sale, my mom finally began to fall out of lockstep with the Program. The Self-Empowerment Training courses had been a gateway for her to other New Age explorations: rebirthing workshops and prosperity seminars among others.

Still, when Mom told me that we were going to drive up to Chicago to see an Indian saint, I was shocked. Although it may have looked Indian from the outside, so much of life in the Movement was about Maharishi and his Vedic vision, not Hinduism. Even more startling to me though was the fact that my mother was going to see someone other than Maharishi for spiritual guidance.

Mom told us that this saint preached a very simple doctrine: universal love. We car-pooled with her friends up to Chicago. Stacey spent the weekend with our dad. On the outskirts of town, we found a small brick Hindu temple, built into a rolling hillside. We joined the crowd of people making their way inside and I was fascinated to see so many Indians—women in saris, men in dhotis, speaking Hindi quickly to each other as they pushed toward the front of the temple. About a hundred or so people had set up blankets and chairs inside. It felt intimate and homey in contrast to the pomp and circumstance of the celebrations for Maharishi in the dome. Someone passed out tea lights to everyone and dimmed the electricity. The crowd began chanting.

Cutting her way through the audience marched a tiny fat Indian woman bundled up in a white sari. This was Ammachi, the Divine Mother. She smiled at everyone and laughed with joy. When people reached out to touch her, she warmly touched them back and even embraced them. A group of swamis in orange robes sat down on the little stage at the front of the room and began playing their instruments. The music was louder and freer than the Gandharva Veda that had become the sound track of our lives at home.

Ammachi sat down in front of a microphone and began singing, her voice throaty and wild. I couldn't help but smile. I loved the idea of an enlightened person who stood right before you and wasn't speaking from another part of the world.

After the music ended, people began jostling against each other and a line formed down the center of the room. Mom pushed us to join in—we were going to receive darshan—the blessing of a saint. I had no idea what this meant—sometimes Mom used Indian terms with me assuming I had a working knowledge of all things Eastern. Before I knew it, we were at the front of the room, and I was sitting just a few feet away from Ammachi. A fan blew on her, and people gathered tightly around, helping her move through the crowd. I watched as she held each person who came to her in a huge bosomy embrace. She whispered into their ears and stroked their hair. Then she would hand them a Hershey's Kiss and they would be off. One of my mom's friends received a dot of sandalwood on his forehead and then his whole body convulsed, as if Ammachi had sent an electric shock through him with her finger.

When it was my time for darshan, I was swept into her arms before I could resist, and she squeezed me to her sari. I was overwhelmed by the smell of sandalwood and rose and incense. She smelled like home. She held me for a long time, stroking my back and whispering in my ear, "Ma, ma, ma, ma, ma." It was like a sweet mother goat sound. I felt my mind go blank the way it did sometimes during my best meditations. I felt—for a moment— nothingness. Darkness. And then I was being gently pushed away. I numbly took my Hershey's Kiss and scooted off the stage to the sidelines.

I watched Mom come down the stage after me, her eyes wet, a big goofy smile on her face. Mom wanted to sit near the stage and stay close to Ammachi while she meditated. I went outside and sat on a little hill near the temple, looking up at the stars. A cute boy with chin-length hair who had an uncanny resemblance to River Phoenix came and sat next to me. He asked if it was my first time seeing Ammachi and he told me about how his parents were hippies and he went to a school in Ohio where they made baskets and handmade soaps. I felt so connected and close to him—*I'm in love!* I thought. Inside the little temple, I could hear the music playing and I felt like I was a part of something vast and important. I wondered if this had been what it had felt like for my mom when she had met Maharishi and learned to meditate.

As we drove home to Fairfield, Mom told me I couldn't tell any of my friends from school what we had done. She told me that the Capital had started to compose a list of people suspected of seeing Ammachi. My friend Ingrid's father, she told me, oversaw this "blacklist." Anyone who goes to see Ammachi won't be allowed back into the dome. I rolled my eyes at her. Why would she want to go to the dome if they were making a blacklist? But I kept her secret; it bound us together. Now we were both hiding something from the Movement: her new devotion and my disbelief.

One evening, I finished reading my latest YA novel and walked down the hallway to my mom's room. She had missed the dome meeting because she was working late and I poked my head inside her bedroom to see if she had finished meditating. She was resting on her bed.

"Hi, Claire-beaux," she said, motioning for me to come lie down beside her. I flopped onto her low bed and curled up against her. I could tell she'd had a good meditation; she seemed soft and sweet. She rubbed my nose gently, running her pointer finger from the top all the way off the little ski jump of the tip. "You have the perfect nose," she said, almost to herself. I closed my eyes and smiled, motioning for her to continue to pet my nose. I loved it when she did this. "I mean I created this nose, and it's absolutely perfect. Not too big, not too small. It doesn't go up at the silly little angle like mine. Your brother's does that a little bit. But not yours. It's perfect."

Feeling close, I decided to confide in her. "I got my period last week." It was quiet and I opened my eyes. My mom was staring at me and then she started laughing.

"God, who are you? You are such a secret keeper! Why didn't you tell me?"

I blushed. It was true that I hadn't really felt like telling my mom. Earlier that year she had bought a box of maxi pads at Walmart and told me she was hiding them under her bathroom sink, "so your brother won't make fun of you." This was the first time my mom had talked to me about the female reproductive system in a formal way. I had a vague memory of her telling me something about magical eggs inside me that dropped out of my body once a month but then that was it.

My mom drew away from me a little and stared at me. "You're so beautiful, honey," she said softly. "You need to be careful."

I didn't quite know what that meant. My mom was always telling me how beautiful I was and I loved it. While my nose was of particular pride for her, she seemed pleased about all of it—my white-blond hair, my small frame, my blue eyes. She acted like I was a marvel. I didn't really care what anyone else thought as long as my mom thought I was beautiful.

At school, after the lunch bell rang, I took my seat in our third-floor classroom. At the front of the room, our teacher Cindy Johnson was talking about a recent meditation experience she had had, in answer to someone's question about one of Maharishi's Fundamentals of Being. As much as we talked here at school about Maharishi and his code for living, and as important as meditation was to everything we did, it was actually rare to hear one of our teachers describe a personal experience of meditation. It felt juicy and gossipy. I leaned forward at my desk to hear her. Ms. Johnson was my favorite teacher, and I could tell that I was one of her favorite students. She seemed to deliver casual witty asides and then sneak a glance at me to see my reaction. When I made a wisecrack, instead of reprimanding me she laughed. I felt like I was in on some private joke with her.

She was very beautiful, like a cross between Princess Diana and Barbie—a curvy figure with blond hair that she always seemed to be raking back with her fingers and haphazardly fixing with little seashell combs. She wore long skirts and fitted sweaters and her students, myself included, were always swirling around her in a devoted sort of hormonal rapture.

"I felt like the walls of the room fell away," she was saying. "There was an orange light and I was consumed by it. I felt boundless, connected to everything. It was the fullest experience of the Unified Field I have ever had." She was blushing as she told the story.

Her description of life-changing, mind-altering meditation was alien to me. My daily experience was humble and simple, at best. At worst, I found myself lost in anxious thought in the solemn silence, imagining worst-case scenarios. What if my mom kicked my brother out of the house? Would Mom lose her new job and if so would we be evicted? It was a far cry from pulsing, overwhelming beams of light and pure being.

It was my birthday that day and Mom had dropped off a small cake. Ms. Johnson asked two of my friends to come up and conduct the cake ceremony, one of the most cherished traditions in the Movement. As the candles were lit, someone would recite in a slow, gentle voice, "On behalf of His Holiness Maharishi Mahesh Yogi we light this light, symbolic of pure consciousness, the light of life for all mankind."

Ms. Johnson handed me the knife and I got to cut the cake, reciting slowly the words to the blessing.

"Cutting the cake is symbolic of action necessary to bring forth the full sunshine of the Age of Enlightenment, Heaven on Earth." I placed the first piece of cake in front of Maharishi's picture at the front of the room. Even though I'd felt pushed away lately by the never-ending flow of philosophy and the cracks in the system, there was something about these words that was mantralike for me. I felt myself for a moment let go, and be lost in reverie. . . . Even though I'd been listening to and saying these little blessings over every cake I'd seen for nearly a decade, the words soothed me. I couldn't help but feel as I went through the motions that I was taking a small step to change the world.

At the same time, I began to have the sense that there was something more real than my life inside the bubble of the Movement. I tried to find out what it was wherever I could—in novels, or in the *Cosmopolitan* magazines that I read in my room when I was supposed to be meditating. Sex and alcohol and desire and crime—all of it felt incredibly alluring to me. At school, my classmates and I exchanged stories like spies in an effort to understand the world beyond what our parents and teachers were telling us.

There were some girls in my class who had no interest in these goings-on—they ate their lunch slowly, sipping hot water, measuring out churnas to balance their doshas. They sat on the grass reading during lunchtime, or went home to be with their mothers—who didn't work—embracing the tenets of an ideal Vedic society at every turn. One such girl was Leah, and she came to embody for me the divide between my new self and the world I was beginning to leave behind. She was contemptuous of my snide negative remarks and would often reprimand me with a quote from Maharishi, one of the slew she seemed to have memorized.

One day in art class, Leah scolded me in her singsong voice for being sarcastic to another girl. "Maharishi says to speak the sweetest truth, Claire."

I turned to her, furious. "Would you jump off a bridge if Maharishi told you to?" I asked.

"Yes," she said, without pause.

I stared at her pale face, her perfectly washed uniform. How could she say that? I turned and walked away, nursing my confusion. Deep down, I envied her confidence. There was a part of me that missed that feeling of absolute trust.

CHAPTER THIRTEEN

Ojas

It can't possibly be how it happened but, as I remember it, hitting puberty for me was like awakening in a music video: suddenly there I was in a Technicolor world bursting with meaning and significance.

What had looked like a wide swath of gray—old snow, dead grass, same old uniforms—had transformed into a color-saturated soap opera. A gaggle of high school girls stood in a circle, laughing loudly, their hands on their hips. Their navy, knee-length uniform skirts were hiked up to midthigh, rolled at the waist to showcase their snow-white-fresh-from-winter legs gleaming in the late afternoon sunlight. In front of them a group of boys had tossed their down coats on the ground and rolled up the sleeves of their collared shirts as they played an animated game of Frisbee. In the parking lot, an old Suburban rattled, engine running, as two girls hung on the door, talking to the lanky kid in the driver's seat. A teenage boy with floppy blond hair, in a trench coat, was leaning against the red Trans Am parked in front of it, blasting The Cure's *"Friday I'm in Love."*

I remember no sex education at the Maharishi School of the Age of Enlightenment. Despite the fact that the Movement was made up largely from a generation that had once shrugged off repressive sexual mores, Maharishi's followers were a strangely earnest and uptight bunch. My mom refused to talk to me about sex. The only mention of sex that I can remember was in an Ayurvedic form I had to fill out when I was twelve years old to assess my dosha balance. It asked me about my sex drive. I showed it to my mom; she was scandalized. I left the answer blank. There was no sex education because there was, of course, no sex being had by teenagers in our Utopia. At least that was the assertion of our enlightened administrators.

The problem with sex was not immorality, but that it was in opposition to the asexual ideal of enlightenment as embodied by our Maharishi. Most of our male teachers seemed to have softened their voices or raised them an octave in an effort to reach a more gender-neutral presence. Women wore knee-length or longer skirts; showing any skin was frowned upon. Maharishi's Indian values of female modesty were upheld, and any behavior that deviated from that was a sign of a lack of balance. So many of Maharishi's teachings were about obtaining a level of consciousness where one had no desires, where one floated around in thoughtless contentment. The twenty-four-hour bliss the TM community was trying to obtain wasn't a sexual one by any means. It was a sober, flat happiness. But, of course, this wasn't the case for teenagers with raging hormones. My moody pubescent state only furthered my sense that I didn't belong to the world of Maharishi's ideal.

Since the boys' and girls' classes were divided, our time together was limited to the hallways and walks to and from PE classes in the field house. This was intended to allow us to focus on developing ourselves as individuals, and toward the shared goal of enlightenment. But outside class, all we seemed to talk about was sex. Who was having it, with whom, and where.

One day after school as I went down to the field house for my JV volleyball practice, the teenage girl who had been working the desk every summer told me about her experience the night before of having sex with two guys at once. My classmates would recount rumors about girls in the upper school sleeping with guys from the college. There were stories of brawls with townies out by the train tracks, fighting over broken hearts and busted relationships. I knew two girls who were sleeping with the fathers of the children for whom they were babysitting.

The dark heart of this furtive sexual energy was a tin shed near the railroad tracks, across the street from an abandoned washing machine factory. It was called the Dojo. Several years before, two meditators—who had kids and went to the dome daily—had started a martial arts studio there. But as the squadron of adolescent boys with black belts hit high school, it had become a den of iniquity. After hours, both the "senseis" and their students were holding wild, alcohol-fueled parties together. In the halls at school, I would hear stories about young teenage girls—thirteen and up—being plied with alcohol there and having sex with the entire Dojo crew. I was warned by adults to stay away but without explanation.

Not that I needed one. I had become defiantly self-protective and self-serving: I was planning my escape from Fairfield. My friend Wells and I would spend long hours talking about the house we would live in together in Los Angeles or New York, and all the cool things we would do, far away from the Movement. I was an opportunist now, looking for ways out. I wasn't going to surrender myself to some group of guys. I wanted to be the user, not the used.

One day my dad came to Fairfield to pick us up for the weekend. He had a serious expression on his face. As we drove out of town, he told us he was moving. "I'm so sorry, you guys. I don't ever want to lose you again. But I can't handle Iowa. I don't want to be a waiter forever. I need to make a real living. And be around artists and writers instead of rednecks." I felt nauseated and sad. I didn't want to be alone here without him. At the same time, I felt something inside me solidify. He'd left before, he was leaving again. That was my dad. He told us he wanted us to come live with him and I gamely agreed, even though I was hurt. But I still wanted to get away. I immediately started plotting. I would move to California, finish high school in Los Angeles with Dad, and get in-state tuition to go to the University of California.

Now that he was at the town school, Stacey left about an hour earlier than me in the mornings, catching the bus at a stop created just for him on the edge of Utopia Park. He wouldn't say much about what happened during the day, although he started calling me the names that kids called him—pillow jockey, guru. Once a kid from school called him at home and I politely said Stacey would call back when he had finished meditating. When Stacey found this out, he gave me a hard shove and told me never to say that again.

Meanwhile, at the Maharishi School, I had begun to flourish socially. I'd started to be invited to slumber parties and after-school hangouts with the rebel girls who, ignoring the gender segregation at school, started hanging out with the boys during recess. I spent less time after school with Genevra, playing make-believe in her mansion, and more time sitting under railroad trestles near the train tracks that cut through Fairfield. Genevra called me on the phone one day during the Program, wanting to know what she had done, but I shrugged it off. I wanted more friends, I told her. I wanted things to be different.

One spring afternoon, as I walked down the path toward the field house in my gym shorts and T-shirt, deep in thought, contemplating whether a) I could be an actress and b) I could make myself cry, I felt a hard thunk on the back of my head. I turned around and saw a group of boys snickering behind me and a Frisbee at my feet. Dougie, Leon, Jiten, and Nick were legends at the school for their rebellious behavior. Nick had recently been suspended for bringing a Chinese throwing star to school and tossing it into the school's air-conditioning system.

Our homeroom teacher, Ms. Johnson, explained that these boys suffered from out of balance "ojas," which she explained was a metaphysical energetic substance that is produced as a result of sex drive being controlled. Too much sex is said to weaken ojas. She said your ojas could be affected from not doing your meditation, touching yourself too much, or eating an excess of garlic and almonds.

These days in PE, our teachers had introduced Maharishi's new health and fitness philosophy, the Invincible Athletics program. This involved sun salutations before working out and lots of pauses to take your pulse and maintain balance. As far as I could tell, the most important thing to do was breathe through your nose and not perspire.

Ms. Johnson shouted from the front of our group, "Claire, get up here right now." I trotted up, blushing. Ms. Johnson reached down and straightened my blouse. "You can see your bra," she said angrily as she adjusted my collar and tightened my red bow tie. I felt shame coming over me. Had I just disturbed the boys' ojas? "Let's focus on the Invincible Athletics program, shall we? Ladies don't talk to men when they're exercising."

Jiten was the smartest kid at school and the funniest. Pale and skinny, with a wild curly Afro, he was different from all his friends. He would tell me stories of all the crazy things they did—drinking, petty crime, fights—but he also made fun of them to me. Ms. Johnson had told me that she thought Jiten and I were the smartest kids in the school, which I knew was totally unprofessional and I loved her for it. Now, thanks to my friendship with Jiten, I had been elevated to some new world of belonging.

I started sneaking out during program time to spend more time with him. We would walk the railroad tracks and sometimes sip from the bottles of MD 20/20, the cheap table wine that he would steal from the local supermarket to get me to make out with him. We spent most of our time making fun of our teachers and our parents' spouses or boyfriends, imitating their sanctimonious voices, parroting Maharishi's knowledge. Then we'd abruptly start making out.

Even as I sneered and rolled my eyes through classes, I did still believe in my teachers' opinions. In my English class, I had started writing ultraviolent miniature fantasy-horror stories. Little children being swooped up by dark beings, husbands and wives assaulting each other. I didn't challenge Maharishi's knowledge directly but I enjoyed writing about a world where it didn't exist.

One day, after reading aloud a short story I'd written about child abduction, my teacher, Mrs. Summers, asked me to stay after class. I felt nervous; I still sought the approval of the adults around me. I sat down at her desk. She was holding my story in her hand.

"You're a writer," she told me. I stared at her. "Did you know that?" she asked gently. Mrs. Summers, red haired, thin, and British, had a reputation for being strict and a hard grader. This was not the lecture on Speaking the Sweet Truth that I had expected. I blushed and shook my head no. "I do like to read . . . ," I offered.

"Well," she said, "I wanted you to know that I can see it. These stories are wonderful." It was the first time I'd been singled out for something special and good. Mrs. Summers handed me two short Hemingway books and sent me down the hall to Sanskrit class.

Not long after, I emerged from the afternoon meditation and walked out into the schoolyard. I found Jiten waiting for me. "How was your meditation?" he asked, mimicking the prissy voice of a teacher. "Was it easy, was it smooth?" I laughed and said I'd been imagining the sex life of our rather shrill meditation teacher, barely remembering my mantra. "All the mantras are the same," he told me, snickering. I laughed, but the idea felt like a missile going through my head. "I thought they were all different, like snowflakes," I said, trying to sound sarcastic. But I was serious; the idea that my mantra was like anyone else's was until that moment inconceivable. "No, tell me yours. I'll bet it's the same as mine," he said. He leaned in close to me, his hand on my arm. His breath warm on my ear, he whispered my mantra in my ear. My mind moved slowly as I looked up at his mischievous grin. I hadn't heard my mantra said out loud for years. Two things occurred to me, and they produced a burst of contradictory feelings. First, that yet another fundamental truth of my meditation had been a lie and that what had felt special for so long was not. And at the same time, I knew that it was our dharma for Jiten and me to be together.

CHAPTER FOURTEEN

Townie

Jiten pulled up outside the trailer and honked the horn. I looked out and saw him sitting in the front seat of his rusted VW Rabbit, his curly hair freshly clipped on the sides, sprouting up into a white-kid version of the Kid 'n Play haircut. We both considered ourselves hip-hop aficionados, spending long afternoons listening to "Three Feet High and Rising" on repeat. Still, I couldn't help but think that his haircut was ill considered—we were about to enter the land of flattops and mullets. I tried to choke down a wave of nausea as I thought about how the two of us would be perceived by the townies. My hair was naturally white-blond—like a fluorescent light on top of my head. I wore it parted far on the side, hiding half my face behind it in a way that I felt was indie and mysterious.

For my first day of high school, I'd chosen a pair of white denim shorts and a blue-and-white polka-dot shirt—an outfit I had thought over long and hard that summer—an all-American look that might just allow me to blend in. My mom frowned at the shortness of my shorts but I ran out the door before she could stop me. I'd just thrown up her homemade whole-wheat carrot-and-raisin muffin in the toilet. I rejected the spoonful of turmeric, Ayurvedic herbs, and honey that she had concocted to soothe me.

I was so nervous that my whole chest was starting to erupt in hives.

Over the summer, Mom had broken the news to me: after the latest tuition hike, she just couldn't afford to send me to the Maharishi School anymore. I would be a freshman at Fairfield High School. I was finally pushed out of the bubble that I had been sullenly occupying for the last few years.

I climbed into the front seat of the car and Jiten started laughing. I was visibly trembling. My chest was bright red. "You'll be fine," he said. "Just act like a townie." We laughed for a second, imagining what that would look like—bangs shellacked in a stiff perm, high-waisted jeans, shouting across the halls with a twang about hog roasts and beers.

After spending the summer locked in each other's sweaty fourteen-year-old embrace, I'd broken up with Jiten at about the same time I'd gotten the news that I'd be going to the town school. Our sexually charged teasing and arguing had turned into something uncomfortable and strange that I couldn't yet handle: intimacy. When he buried his head in my lap one day after his stepfather had thrown a bowl of steaming-hot broccoli at him—while his mother had done nothing—I felt repulsed. I knew how Jiten felt—we both had endured years of lame guys weaving in and out of our mothers' lives. But his softness and sadness pushed me away. I didn't want to be weak, and I didn't want my boyfriend to be weak.

I broke up with him the next day. He sat in the front seat of his car, tears running down his cheeks. Later that night, he appeared at my window, begging me to come back. This only made it worse. We continued to spend all our time together but instead of fiendishly making out during program time, we took long walks along the railroad tracks, contemplating what the fall was going to bring us, what life would be like outside the Oz-like land we'd grown up in. Jiten had told his parents that he wanted to go to the town school—many of his friends at the Maharishi School had been expelled and he was tired of being treated like a degenerate.

Jiten didn't seem to care at all about being different. He already belonged to a crew of older guys from the Dojo who were juniors and seniors at Fairfield. They served as a sort of mafia, granting him protection and immunity from the hostility the townies felt toward the followers of Maharishi. But I felt I had no protection. Stacey had no interest in talking to me, let alone sticking up for me. He had given me a few terse words of advice—don't talk about meditation, don't talk to him.

I tried to impersonate Jiten's brash stare as we parked the car near the football field and walked toward the concrete steps with the hundreds of other kids. Outside, the air was heavy with the smell of freshly mowed grass. Fairfield High School looked like a monolithic, prisonlike structure. It was three stories high, with small windows and a large American flag flapping in the breeze. Inside the dim fluorescent-lit hallways, the acrid smell of bleach and disinfectant stung my nostrils. The stone stairs were gleaming, and swarms of kids moved past us in great waves. The seniors looked like giants—football players with calves the size of tree trunks. And the girls, with their permed hair and shellacked bangs and big rowdy laughter, seemed brazen and intense.

This was a far cry from the dimly lit hallways of the Maharishi School, where everyone spoke in soft, sweet tones. Despite my misgivings about Maharishi's program, I had been able to blend in there; no one paid me much mind.

The white shorts, it turned out, were a bad idea. Football players, wrestlers, guys from the agricultural club—they all paused to talk to me, some even touched my hair as I walked past them in the halls. I tried to keep my head down, and hide my face, which was now tomato red.

The rough behavior of the public school kids felt abrasive to me—they shoved each other in the hall; guys groped the girls, shouting insults to their friends, their voices echoing off the brick walls. At the Maharishi School, if a kid yelled—a sign of unstressing and imbalance—he quickly would have been reprimanded in a gentle but firm tone. Maharishi's wisdom would've been invoked, as well as a larger, cosmic sense of disapproval.

When I came home that day, our phone started ringing and didn't stop for hours. My mom smirked at me as she hung up the phone on yet another guy, after giving our agreed-upon excuse. "They just want to get to know you better," she laughed. Within two weeks, sixteen different guys had asked me to the homecoming dance. With each one, I quietly mumbled that I couldn't, backing away, hoping they wouldn't shout out something that would draw more attention to me. All I wanted to do was disappear. And all this male attention meant that I had absolutely no chance of making new female friends. After a day or two, even Jiten lost patience and stopped offering me a ride to school. The girls that I dared to make eye contact with as I walked past whispered, "Fucking slut." Or they would briskly shove me into a locker and keep walking. Those first months, the tires on Mom's rusted station wagon were slashed and, more than once, we woke up to find our trailer coated in eggs.

I plowed through my days, clutching the little mimeographed computer printout of my classes that the guidance counselor had given me on the first day. It all felt so industrial and impersonal. Everywhere I turned, I felt hard faces staring at me.

As the weeks went on, I did make one new friend. Heather was a bubbly, jockish girl who sat next to me in English class, and considered herself broad-minded. She was dating one of the Vietnamese refugee kids who had come to Fairfield in the seventies sponsored by the Methodist church. Within minutes of introducing herself, Heather told me my problem was that I didn't have any friends, which was why everyone was picking on me. Her boyfriend, Tou, who was a foot shorter than she was, played every sport, drove a truck, pegged his jeans in a tight roll at the ankle, and was easily one of the most beloved kids at the five-hundred-person high school. She told me I needed to stop staring at the ground in the hallway and, like Tou, start being friendly to people.

One day she offered to eat lunch with me—a step up from the forty minutes I usually spent hiding in the bathroom stall with my whole-wheat sandwiches. Heather walked me through the lunch line, and I stared in amazement at the sloppy joe concoction that the plastic-capped lunch server threw on my plate. Heather guided me over to a table of frizzy-haired girls who wore Champion T-shirts and Guess blue jeans. "This is Claire," Heather said. "She's pretty cool." There was silence and then slowly the girls started introducing themselves. It felt like I had passed through an invisible door.

As I was learning to love pigs in a blanket and tightly pegged jeans, Maharishi stepped up his global efforts in the 1990s. He was no longer satisfied with our community and the simple pursuit of Enlightenment or Perfect Health or an Ideal Society. In the midnineties, Fairfield experienced an economic boom with the emergence of several extremely successful telecommunications businesses created by local meditators. In 1997, *Wired* magazine dubbed Fairfield and this crop of telecommunications companies the "Silicorn Valley" of America, reporting the estimated value of one of the companies at $300 million. The owners of two such companies, both of whom were devoted meditators, paid homage to Maharishi, and his 200 percent vision of life, in the form of large monetary donations.

This created a material renaissance for Fairfield, as large amounts of money poured into the university. Suddenly, it seemed everyone had work. My mom got a promotion at her job with the local telecommunications company; her benefits package even included discounted prices on Ayurvedic treatments at the local spa, The Raj. Just as this economic growth took hold, Maharishi announced his plan to rebuild the entire world using Sthapatya Veda doctrine.

According to Maharishi, Sthapatya Veda was one of the forty aspects of the Vedas that delineated the principles of architecture, environmental design, and planning. "Maharishi Mahesh Yogi has revived Sthapatya Veda as a precious discipline of his Vedic Science and Technology program, the science and technology of consciousness, and restored the dignity of this timeless knowledge by re-enlivening its connection with the Unified Field," read the promotional materials that were suddenly everywhere—printed and distributed by the newly established local company, Maharishi Global Construction.

Everything became about aligning structures with nature. And that alignment had a name: "Vastu," the "spatial orientation aligned to Natural Law." Rebuilding the world was an ambitious project, but of course, Maharishi had thought through the details. He had mapped out a grid of global roads that would run true north and true south according to the cardinal directions.

Within his global design, there were plans for new buildings and homes in Fairfield. The Heaven on Earth Development Corporation, another Maharishi-affiliated company, presented to the media plans to create Maharishi ideal communities that would ring each of the great cities of the world, like a cosmic life jacket.

Maharishi Sthapatya Vedic buildings had a distinct look to them, pastel-colored with a large flame-shaped ornament on the top. Inside there was a hollow core or atrium called the Brahmasthan. This hollow space was meant to be a model of the unified field, a space of individual transcendence where the laws of nature aligned and a holistic balance came into existence, resulting in "proper Vastu." This harmony would inspire a radiative effect, the "Vastu Effect," which in turn would effect manifestations in the material life of the owner, creating prosperity and health. The Vastu Effect, much like the Maharishi Effect, brought us closer to the establishment of World Peace and Heaven on Earth.

Entering a building from the south was dangerous, Maharishi decreed, and could conjure up negativity and rakshasas, dark demons. Overnight, every meditator changed the entrance to their homes to avoid this negativity. Mom deemed the front door of our house, which faced the street, "the back door." We were asked to no longer use it. The entrance to campus—which was for decades to the south—was barricaded. The fishponds, once the prettiest part of the campus, were filled with mud and fenced off because Maharishi had recently decided water might also bring the rakshasas. The sweet little stone cathedral with the stained glass windows was torn down and replaced with a yellow prefab rectangular building from Maharishi Global Construction.

But Maharishi's ambitions extended further. He soon announced his plans for a billion-dollar fund-raising campaign to erect the tallest buildings in the world. Slated for a number of cities, including

São Paulo, Brazil, these buildings would be different from the other gargantuan skyscrapers of urban skylines. Maharishi's would be a gigantic, 108-story pyramid, resembling an ancient Vedic temple (the number chosen, just like the name of Maharishi's group of wealthy donors, for its sacred connotation). At the top of the 1,622-foot building—housing offices, shops, and a university—would be a restaurant that from the outside looked like a giant golden crown. Even in Fairfield, it was possible to feel the shadowy strain of the Maharishi's need for ever-greater financial resources to implement his ever-greater ambitions.

As the Movement seemed to be moving toward something radically more Vedic, I was moving swiftly in the other direction, trying my hardest to be a true-blue American teenager. After years at the Maharishi School feeling on the edge of belonging, I was more than ready to embrace my new world. I admired the seeming ease with which my townie friends went about their lives—intentionally acting stupid or rude, making scatological jokes, generally behaving without a care (or ambition) in the world. They blared Metallica and Billy Ray Cyrus and got hammered. My new friends weren't running from anything or trying to change the past or willing themselves to be a little brighter and a little better. They were comfortable with the way things were and that was fine.

But I also feared their fearlessness, and still felt safest with my meditator friends from the Maharishi School—Ananda, Wells, Ingrid, and Joey—and started taking them to football games and wrestling matches, becoming their conduit into the great unknown. We would laugh at the crass jokes that the kids in the bleachers would make and flip our hair, eyes full of innuendo and irony. We went to house parties in parts of town I'd never even seen, drinking wine coolers on shag carpets, while Midwestern mothers smoked cigarettes, the TV blaring as they cooked large trays of mystery meat in the kitchen. I drank Gatorade, ate Cheetos, and guzzled down Coors Zimas. For a while, I stopped meditating altogether.

None of them had become as cynical about the Movement as I had. We agreed that their teachers were uptight and that many of the people on campus acted like zombies. They had become as bored as I was with the constant edicts of Ideal Vedic Living. But none of them really questioned whether Maharishi was a good person or not.

This was something I had started to think about a lot. Did Maharishi even know about us? I knew that sometimes during dome celebration telecasts, he would look out at us and laugh. But did he know about Utopia Park and scholarship students? Did he know that the price of tuition was going up and that kids like me were being forced out? Or that people like my mom had to scrimp and save to be able to go to the dome and practice the meditation that he said would change the world? I'd hear my mom's friends repeat the same quote from Maharishi over and over again: Americans only value things if they have to pay for them. There was something condescending about the way he called us Americans. It felt truly sacrilegious to say anything bad about Maharishi to my mom or any of the other adults. But even if I made a joke to my friends about Maharishi wanting more money or being jealous of other gurus, they made it clear that I had gone too far.

I was living on the edges of two worlds, not quite belonging to either one. I envied my friends from the Maharishi School who didn't have to deal with being the weirdo at school. As much as I'd felt suffocated by the restrictions and the striving at the Maharishi School, I missed the safety.

My perverse response was to push further. I started to take risks. The small shoplifting infractions that had begun at the campus bookstore grew to be a constant habit at department stores in Iowa City. I started drinking every weekend, alcohol that we would stuff down our pants at the local grocery store. The deviance felt like a relief even as it increased my anxiety.

Mostly, though, I felt numb. And the only way to shake off that feeling was to break what felt like the million rules that surrounded me. Breaking the rules felt really, really good. The first time I sneaked out of Utopia Park my heart was hammering in my chest, in my ears, in my neck, in my nose, every part of me throbbing with fear. But Ingrid and I had made a plan, and she, the braver of us two by far, was suddenly there, outside my window on that summer night, her low voice chuckling, her big brain completely caught up in our subterfuge.

I slipped out of the window easily, that wasn't a problem. The trailer was so low to the ground that I'd occasionally used it as an entrance and exit as a kid, pushing the screen out and wiggling out on my belly till my toes touched the grass. And then we were off, through the maze of trailers, past Taste of Utopia Street, out onto Heavenly Lane, until finally we were off campus.

Somebody or other was there to pick us up. We felt like we were all breathing nitrogen, giddy and squeaky-voiced with what we had done by opening the door out of our rigid consciousness-based life. I was leaving consciousness behind.

We drove out of town along the back roads until we hit a small highway that ran south of town. It was early summer and the warmth of the day was hitting the cool of the night, creating long clouds of fog that we drove through. It felt like the tall meadows and cornfields were exhaling these puffs of gray steam. We all groaned as we passed a pig farm, the sharp, bitter scent choking us. We held our breaths.

Mostly we talked about getting caught: how it would happen, what we would say, how we would be punished. For my friends from the Maharishi School, getting thrown out of school loomed large but for me it was about disappointing my mom, and destroying the illusion of being the easy, well-behaved kid.

We pulled up to the quarry alongside a few other cars. Just past the parking lot, in a clearing amid the tall meadow grasses, a few older kids from MSAE had built a bonfire. I was the last one to climb out, tugging down my jeans shorts and staring up at the sky. The huge inky blackness was filled with more stars than I had ever seen, so bright that they looked like ornaments dangling down in front of my face. I was pulled inward and yearned to be alone with the stars, away from everyone else.

But, being fifteen, I tried to ignore that impulse. I walked up to the group and happily accepted the beer tossed my way. We sat around for a while, talking mostly about crazy stuff going on at school and on campus. I felt a little on the edge of the conversation. My old friends were in high school now, with new teachers. I hadn't had to take all the Sanskrit or do the Rising Siddhi program, or any of the other weird new iterations of Maharishi's knowledge that they complained about.

"I'm going for a swim," I announced to no one in particular. I walked down to the gravelly edge of the water and stripped down to my underwear. I checked the edges for water moccasins, their long thick bodies being one of my primary fears in life, and then waded in. I was a confident if not talented swimmer, and I paddled my way out to the center of the quarry. I tried not to think about what I'd heard—that the water was so deep, at the bottom there was a huge dump filled with cars, forklifts, and other machinery lost from another time. I flipped over and floated on my back, finally alone with the stars. The water was still warm from the day's heat and it felt like being in an enormous bathtub. All I could hear was the water lapping in my ears and my own breath. Without thinking, I started saying my mantra gently to myself, keeping my eyes open and fixed on the vastness of the sky.

For a moment, I felt it. That feeling of infinity and unity. Maybe there was a Unified Field, just like Maharishi said, some primordial cosmic space from which everything had sprung. And maybe my mantra was dialing me into its frequency so that I could just be here, a small speck, humming along with its rhythm.

After six months at FHS, I was slogging my way through class barely surviving. Mostly, this meant that I had a place to sit during lunch hour, and that no one had thrown my body against a locker in recent weeks or slashed my mom's tires. But in gym class, I felt whatever shred of integration I had managed ripped away.

At the Maharishi School, we all sort of blended into a continuum of limited ability that was solidified by our single-sex gym classes. Maharishi had announced that girls should not sweat, so those classes were never particularly rigorous. We took our pulse, we did sun salutes, and then we took a walk or played a slow game of kick ball. At the end, we would take our pulse again and talk about our doshas.

In the Fairfield High School gym class, I felt like I was in the WNBA. Most of the girls had been playing softball and basketball and volleyball since they could walk; their bodies were muscular in a way I had literally never seen before. There was also a whole new world of "sports" that I had not encountered: gun safety, fishing, archery, and bowling (with an emphasis on scorekeeping). In the locker room, I was surrounded by a swarm of glittering caramel-colored torsos—fresh from tanning beds—and ample haunches clad in Victoria's Secret thongs.

One day, two of the more popular freshman girls, Tiffany and Amanda, were showing off the little Playboy bunny tattoos above their pubic hairline created by putting a sticker there before going into the tanning bed. I tried to keep my eyes to myself as I trudged over to my locker and opened my backpack. Their bodies were a far cry from the thin white vegetarian frames of the Maharishi kids I'd grown up with. I pulled out my gray shorts and graying white shirt that I'd bought at Walmart with my babysitting money. I had created my own school uniform: five T-shirts, two pairs of jeans, one gym outfit. I also had a pair of no-name tennis shoes that were the bane of my existence, as clear a marker as any that I had arrived straight from Utopia Park.

I tried to pull my clothes on and off as quickly as possible so that no one would catch a glimpse of my soft white body. But, on that day, I heard a loud, rough voice call out to me from across the room. "Hey, Claire, I heard you guys had fun on Saturday night!" All other conversation stopped. My stomach rolled over inside and my entire face caught fire.

That Saturday night I had gone on my first real townie date. I had known ahead of time that this was not a smart move if I wanted to go unnoticed. And yet I had a huge crush on a guy named Joe and practically swooned when he asked me in the school corridor if I wanted to go to a party with him that weekend. In my heart, I knew that I could never really love anyone who wasn't a meditator. How could anyone who didn't grow up with a mantra understand who I was? But I wasn't looking for love or anything close. I liked the idea of breaking a taboo. Dating a townie made a bold statement: I was crossing over to the other side.

On the night of our date, I lay in my bed, the lights out, listening for the sounds of my family falling asleep. I'd always been a night owl, staying up late and reading underneath the covers by the light of my alarm clock. I loved listening to the quiet sounds of a Midwestern night: the cicadas chirping; the rustle of the tall elm trees outside my window; the gentle wind pushing against the metal of the trailer. I savored the freedom of being alone in my room, able to read or think or imagine whatever I wanted.

Now this freedom meant I could sneak out. There was a tap on my window, and my heart began to pound—was it too loud? I rolled over and pushed up the thin sash. Again, Ingrid stood there, tall, with her long hair reaching to the middle of her back. Her voice was very deep and very loud. "Claire bear!" she began to whisper, but I shushed her. It sounded like a sonic boom from inside the quiet of the trailer.

I grabbed my shoes—a pair of black Chinese buckle slippers—and dropped them out the window. Next to my bed was a copy of *Roots*, which my teacher at Fairfield High had allowed me to read after I finished the year's textbook in the first month. Inside the pages, I kept a folded, carefully written note: "Dear Mom, Ingrid came by and she was super stressed out. We have gone for a Walk and Talk. Back soon. Love, Claire."

I pushed my legs out the window, and scooted down the side of the trailer on my stomach. Ingrid was standing there, a huge grin on her face, trying not to laugh. I slipped my shoes on and we ran through the trailers. The clear stars overhead in the sky gave the night an amplified sense of magic.

We ran until we reached the edge of campus, and then walked along the local reservoir. We stopped once we got to the graveyard, then found a place to sit in the shadows. A long willow tree created an ideal cover. Headlights lit up the grass in front of us and we peeked out from the branches to see Joe's truck. We raced from our hiding spot, and crawled inside the car where we were greeted with high fives and howls. Joe had three of his friends from the wrestling team with him and they had all been drinking. There was nowhere to sit but on their laps, and we wriggled around trying to seem as light and small as possible. "We're going to go to a hog roast, ladies!" one kid shouted. The guys made squealing sounds.

I thought Joe's friends were sketchy and dumb, but I was willing to ignore it. I wanted to focus on Joe. He was a wiry wrestler, not particularly large, but with a mop of dark brown hair and sleepy eyes. He didn't say much, which allowed me to project all sorts of deep emotions and qualities on him that even I, deep down, suspected weren't really there.

We drove toward the edge of town, where we picked up two more girls from the Maharishi School. They piled into the car, primly finding a space between the wrestlers. We turned onto a dirt road I'd never been on before—this was a part of town where meditators didn't live. Joe turned up John Cougar Mellencamp on the radio, drowning out the sound of his tires on the gravel. Somebody rolled down the front windows, and the fresh, earthy smell of ponds came in. I closed my eyes and let the air hit my face.

Joe pulled his truck into a field crowded with pickups, and we piled out. At the center of a field, a huge bonfire was blazing. Someone had their truck stereo blasting Metallica and there were kegs of beer on the ground. Joe gallantly chaperoned us through the staring crowd. Our straight hair, our shyness, all of it betrayed that we were from the weird part of town. Above us, a full moon shined bright. Kids on four-wheelers raced past. Ingrid nudged me—the carcass of a massive pig was hanging on a nearby tree.

"Ewww," I screeched, and Joe took that opportunity to put his short, muscled arm around me for a kiss. I felt oddly removed from what was happening, overwhelmed by the smell of Budweiser and pig flesh and cigarettes.

Next to me Ingrid and the other girls had been talked into some sort of drinking game. I caught glimpses of them guzzling beer from red plastic cups. After a little while, I saw a few of them disappear into the bushes with a group of guys. I felt embarrassed. I didn't want the kids from the town school to think we were sluts. But the next thing I knew, Joe was leading me off to the woods, his arm wrapped tight around my waist. He pushed me against a tree, his body pressed against mine, his arms working over me with expert ease, quickly trying to undress me. I felt suddenly totally out of my league—I'd been swept away by it all—the classic rock, the beer, the rowdy libertine freedom of everyone around me. But I didn't know this guy who was trying to get me naked and my friends had all disappeared. As Joe was going to work on removing my jeans, Amanda and Tiffany, two townie girls sauntered up, accompanied by their football-player boyfriends. I quickly buttoned my pants. Joe turned to greet them, high-fiving them and laughing. He didn't look at me as he took a beer from one of the guys, and neither of the girls spoke to me.

While some part of me had thought being part of the Movement and having parents with advanced degrees meant that I was above them, they saw me as an outsider, a disposable girl. They would go on to marry each other and build lives together; I was just an easy blonde from a trailer park. I waited quietly for Joe to take me home.

That Monday, inside the locker room, I feigned nonchalance. "Yeah," I said, "we got hammered." I had never used the word before and it sort of fell off my tongue. The two girls exchanged glances. Who had I been kidding that I could belong to the townie world? Soon Joe had stopped speaking to me, walking past me in the hall like he didn't know me. I returned to a lunch table at the far end of the cafeteria, where a few kids who had transferred from the Maharishi School sat together, eating quietly with our backs turned against the boisterous world of nonmeditators.

To make matters worse though, among my Maharishi School friends, I'd become known as a kid who ran fast and loose with the townies. So that summer when Ingrid and several other friends were told they would not be allowed to learn to fly because of their bad reputations, their parents trained their eyes on me. The Rising Siddha program was a fundamental part of being an upper school student at the Maharishi School. When you turned sixteen, you were allowed to get your Siddhis, which included the flying technique. After two decades of pouring time and money into the Movement, these parents were devastated to have their kids rejected. When I first went to Ingrid's house after she'd gotten the news, she coached me on what to say to her mom. "Don't say anything bad about the Movement, okay? And also make sure you tell her that you switched to the town school because you couldn't afford it."

I blushed. "No, I switched because I didn't like the Maharishi School."

"Don't say that," she said. "Whatever you do, don't criticize it."

From then on, my presence at her house felt strange. Her parents, though they seemed to like me, feared my influence, my vaguely townie air.

I had cobbled together my own reality. I felt stuck between those two worlds—the townies and the 'rus. I wasn't either one, though I could successfully pretend in both. I could cross over by rolling up my T-shirt sleeves and drinking a beer, or I could speak slowly with lots of eye contact and assure meditators that I was still one of them, that I knew what god consciousness was and still aspired to it. But I felt confused about who I was. I really didn't belong anywhere and it was then that I started to form the idea that my identity was that of an outsider.

Where I felt most myself was during my weekly phone calls with my dad. He encouraged me to tell him about the kids at school, what I was doing. He loved hearing about the townies and their redneck ways and my descriptions of Maharishi's plans to rebuild the world. He would laugh at my stories, as if I was living in the funniest place in the world. He'd send back hand-drawn cartoons and short plays that showed me as a puffy-haired diva, sophisticated and spoiled, who could barely be bothered by the rednecks and the weirdos who surrounded her. "It's such a great story," he would say, and by those lights it felt like this was just a temporary chapter that would soon come to a close.

CHAPTER FIFTEEN

Meth Heads and Meditators

The sun was just starting to set and Utopia Park glowed pink in the twilight. Tall grasses grew between the maze of trailers. A group of friends had dropped me off on the edge of campus—we had been out celebrating on the last day of our sophomore year—so I would have a few minutes to walk home by myself. It was nine o'clock at night—my curfew—and I'd taken the mushrooms an hour before. My plan was to go home, say as brief a good night as possible, and then get to my room in time to sneak out before I was fully tripping.

On campus, Maharishi's administration was bulldozing all the old buildings and replacing them with golden-colored office buildings that looked like they should be in a business park in Calcutta. They all had the requisite columns and the golden spires on the top. Maharishi would soon ask that instead of having his devotees live in the town of Fairfield—as they had for decades—those who truly wanted to achieve Enlightenment would move to his newly incorporated Vedic City, which sat on the outskirts of town. Houses there—constructed according to his trademarked technology and design—would cost more than twice what the houses cost in town.

My mom had stopped going to the dome. Instead, she meditated at home and then listened to tapes by Ammachi. Stacey had moved out. He had graduated from high school, but despite my parents' protestations, decided to skip college. He'd hitchhiked to Mexico where he started working in a seafood restaurant and lived on the beach in Oaxaca. We got postcards from him occasionally. Far away from all the craziness, he seemed happy for the first time, and I could detect a softness that moved me to forgive him for his years of teasing me. With Stacey no longer around, a certain relaxation had set in at home.

Mom even liked my latest boyfriend, Nick—though she had no idea what a terrible influence he was. With her, he was polite and attentive, always asking questions and calling her ma'am and "Mrs." He had pale skin and green eyes and was one of the more popular kids at Fairfield High School, which was saying something since he was a meditator. (He'd been expelled from the Maharishi School in eighth grade after a series of infractions—stealing alcohol, dirty drawings, talking back.) He was one of Jiten's best friends, and had a black belt in karate. Nick coexisted happily with the townies; he was a jock with a deeply obscene sense of humor. Everyone seemed to love him.

Nick was all about pushing the boundaries and he kept upping the ante for our circle of former Maharishi School friends, who were all at Fairfield High because we'd either been priced out or because of "nonideal" behavior. Nick was casually dealing weed and mushrooms to the townies and to college kids at the Maharishi International University. I had started smoking pot during Program time with him and Ingrid, while my mom meditated. It was also with Nick and Ingrid that I had munched a bag of crusty mushrooms earlier that evening. Now, I could feel them starting to take effect, the edges of my vision starting to whorl.

I walked up the wooden steps and opened the sagging screen door to our trailer. Inside, Mom was making herself an herbal tea and sweeping the cracked linoleum kitchen floor. She greeted me warmly, and despite my better judgment, I sprawled onto the old living room chair—with its polyester fabric hardened like wax. "How was your day?" I asked. She started to tell me about how she'd fought with her manager, how she'd had her feelings hurt by the way he'd spoken to her. I found myself interested in a way that I hadn't been in years. Slowly, the trailer started to melt around the edges and I kept trying to blink it away. Mom laughed at my spaced-out attitude. "You are a real weird kid, Claire-beaux," she said. I knew that was my cue to get out. I gave her a hug, thankful that mushrooms didn't have a smell, and went to my bedroom.

Twenty minutes later, I was walking with Ingrid along a dirt path, on our way to go skinny-dipping. As we walked, I felt like my eyes were opening for the first time, and that I was seeing the world anew. Everything felt so beautiful, just as it should've been. I felt an incredible sense of ease and euphoria.

Ingrid and I were holding hands, tears streaming down our cheeks as we realized together that this was what our parents had been pursuing all these years. A feeling you could get from some cruddy mushrooms in a Ziploc bag! Practically every parent I knew at the Maharishi School had ended up learning TM in college, usually after taking psychedelic drugs. Maharishi had promised that TM would give them that same high, naturally. But this feeling, this wild, exalted sense of happiness, this wasn't something we'd ever felt before. "Cosmic consciousness?" Ingrid said, and we wept elated tears. We were glimpsing the nirvana that our lives had been contorted toward for as long we knew.

Nick had transferred to FHS the same year I had. Right away, he dated an athletic local girl named Jackie and she was madly in love with him. At some point, Jackie and Nick had a tumultuous breakup. Not long after, Nick's constant teasing of me transitioned into something else. Suddenly *we* were madly in love. He had intimidated me for years, and when he focused his sweet side on me, I crumbled. For all his wildness, he was almost a parody of a good boyfriend. He brought me roses for no reason. He would come eat dinner at our house, complimenting my mom on her cooking as he washed the dishes.

After their breakup, his ex-girlfriend showed up at school with "luv sux" carved into her arm with a razor blade. She wept openly when she saw me, or ran in the other direction, her long brown hair a witchy swoosh behind her. I now had the scariest of enemies—a wild-eyed heartbroken sixteen-year-old girl.

One day, when Nick came to pick me up from school, he told me that Jackie had come to his house with a kitchen knife and tried to stab him while he was sleeping. Then when he grabbed her, she tried to stab herself.

Not long after, one early spring morning in my sophomore year, Jackie walked past me in the hall and shrieked, "You are a fucking bitch." I kept walking but my heart was pounding. I tried to say my mantra as I made my way to biology class but my mind was racing too fast. Although I had always trusted that I had an inner coherence, that I could keep my calm no matter what, now I felt I was losing control of my temper. My body was shaking. What was wrong with me? I said my mantra over and over in my head, clinging to it like a raft.

After class Jackie brushed past me in the hallway and then threw her books down, screaming. She grabbed my hair and I felt something inside me snap. I'd spent the last two years being bullied at this school. I'd tried to act like a cool enlightened meditator, focused on some greater destiny and trying not to care about their small-town bullshit. But right now I cared and I was furious.

With her still holding on to my hair I turned around and punched her hard in the face. She fell down fast, dragging me on top of her as she kept her clutch on my hair. I kept punching her face, over and over. A tight perimeter of kids formed around us, laughing and cheering. I was probably the first meditator to get into a girl fight and the crowd loved it.

The next thing I knew two teachers were dragging me off Jackie, pulling me toward the principal's office. As quickly as my violent urges had begun, they subsided. Immediately, I felt like my old self—desperately wanting to escape the eyes of the people gaping at me in the hall. Someone marched Jackie past me, her face bleeding, as she screamed out wild sobs. Within minutes, the principal informed me I was suspended. My mom pulled up in front of the school, where I sat on the steps feeling gloomy. I got in the car and she stared at me.

"Are you okay?" she asked. I said yes, and saw that her eyes had started watering a little. Then she started laughing, hard.

"What?" I said.

"Just my little Claire-beaux, getting into fights!" To her, it was so out of character that she didn't take it seriously. But I was anxious about my record. Had I just ruined my chances of going to college? Would I be stuck forever in Fairfield because I'd let some dark part of me take over? Had I become a townie?

A few weeks later, for reasons that I still cannot understand, my mom agreed to let me drive up to Minneapolis one weekend with Nick to visit his father. I had just gotten my driver's license three days earlier and I was thrilled. When Nick pulled up in front of our trailer that morning, he just honked his horn instead of coming inside, which seemed odd. My mom was working at her drawing table and waved me off, telling me to be careful.

I scampered out and opened the passenger-side door, throwing my backpack in the back. Nick's face, which was normally vampire white, was red and blotchy. As he drove out of Utopia Park he regaled me with the story of his wild night—he'd done five hits of acid and gone to a bar in Keosauqua—a rural community twenty miles away. I saw now that his pupils were hugely dilated. He said he might still be tripping, so I insisted on driving, even though my time behind the wheel had been limited almost entirely to driver's ed. Nick agreed easily, climbed over to the passenger seat, and immediately passed out.

We'd gone about forty-five miles, heading north on the five-hour drive to Minnesota, when I decided to pull over to pee. Nick was sleeping soundly next to me, and I downshifted clumsily. In the rearview mirror I saw a huge car-transporter truck barreling down behind me, and I took a quick left toward the gas station on the other side of the highway, at which point our engine stalled. Frantically, I pushed my foot on the clutch to start the car again but the next thing I knew I heard a terrible sound and everything went black. When I opened my eyes, I was surrounded by cars in every direction. I looked to my right, and in the passenger seat I saw blood dripping down the side of Nick's head.

I woke up again inside an ambulance, strapped to a gurney. A woman lying next to me was wailing about the stupid idiot who had pulled in front of her and how she had three kids in the car and how she was going to sue my ass off. She wouldn't stop yelling and I could see blood on her face. I closed my eyes. I wasn't hurt—in fact I was totally fine—but, at that moment, I hoped that somehow I would die. The idea of how much all of this was going to cost made me feel dizzy. I started saying my mantra slowly in my head, trying to lose myself in black nothingness. I passed out again, into a traumatized oblivion.

When my mom arrived at the hospital she was furious, growling about how we did not have money to pay for hospital bills and car accidents. I kept silent, hating myself more than she ever could. Nick had already left with his grandmother—he had a head injury but she had likely sensed his intoxicated state and gotten him out of sight as fast as possible. Thankfully, the woman in the hospital bed next to me was fine, as were her kids. She had however broken her nose and she wanted me to buy her a new car. I sat in the backseat of my mom's station wagon on the way home, pretending to sleep. She worked out a deal with Nick where she would pay the court, I would pay the cost of replacing the woman's car and he would handle everything else. It felt like the worst day of my life.

Not long after that, Mom came home with a flyer announcing a summer program in Washington, D.C., called Group for a Government. Maharishi had set up a program to use the Maharishi Effect to transform the capital from one of the most murderous cities in America to one of its most peaceful. He was asking meditators from Fairfield and around the world to spend the summer in the capital, meditating for six or more hours a day, thus radiating their peaceful transformative energy.

Maharishi declared Washington, D.C., a "pit of mud" at a press conference, which turned out to be a setup for another Maharishi initiative: the Natural Law Party. Maharishi announced that the American political system was a failure and that his Movement had organized a political platform that used meditation to solve the ills of the country. The principles of SCI were woven into the campaign language.

Mom pointed to the bottom of the flyer. It read, "Call Patty about the Super Radiance Children's Summer Camp. Camp counselors wanted." "This could be a way for you to make that money," she said. I dutifully walked through the trailers to Patty's house—her son Benj had been a classmate at the Maharishi School—and got the job.

The Super Radiance camp was housed at Gallaudet, a university for the hearing impaired in Washington, D.C. When we arrived, a few students who hadn't left yet for the summer watched with interest as we unloaded carloads of foam and "back-jacks," for meditating.

I shared a room with Gen, a high school senior who had recently come to Fairfield from Canada. We spent every moment together, her yearning for her boyfriend and me yearning to leave Iowa. (After the accident, things had cooled between me and Nick; we broke up when I left for Washington.)

Every morning, at 7 a.m., we would trudge downstairs to the dining hall and assume control of our students while their parents rushed off for the group-flying program. Half of them flung their children at us, frantic to make it in time. The others would go over long lists of allergies and special needs. We learned the doshas of our wards, and whether they were in balance or not. For some, we were given a schedule for their herbal supplements. I could have sworn that even Mr. Eyre, a longtime teacher from the Maharishi School, rolled his eyes at ten-year-olds showing up with their own little flasks of Amrit Kalash, the sticky so-called nectar of the gods sold by Maharishi Ayurveda Products International.

After the Word of Wisdom, we'd practice the Veda Lila, a song and play that Maharishi had written. I had practiced the Veda Lila so many times as an elementary school student that I could've sung it in my sleep.

Using my best, most solemn voice, I began to sing:

One unbounded ocean of consciousness in motion
in waves of creation flowing, an ocean of knowingness,
an ocean of consciousness

I carved out the waves of the ocean of consciousness with my arms, while also hissing out the side of my mouth at the eight-year-old boys who were making funny faces at each other. I led the children through the Ved, pantomiming the different aspects of Vedic knowledge and then unifying into one transcendent whole. I could also do this in my sleep. We finished the finale high pitched, like we were all actresses in a Bollywood movie.

The Samhita, of Rishi, Devata and Chandas
the togetherness of three in one reality
In one unbounded ocean of consciousness
One appears as three while remaining unity

We always took a respectful moment of silence at the end—supposedly performing the Veda Lila had its own transcendent effects. It felt strange teaching these kids something that I had never really enjoyed myself. It didn't make much sense to me—I didn't really know what the "samhita" was, and all the hand motions of three becoming one, well, it was just odd. The familiarity of it, the spooky, slow way you sang it did make you sort of stop thinking about anything else. But I wasn't sure that was a good thing. As I watched the little faces looking up at me, trying to follow along, stumbling over the "samhita," I felt like a hypocrite. Why were we doing it if none of us knew what it meant?

Back in Fairfield that winter, when I was sixteen years old, I talked on the phone with my dad several times a week, cooking up schemes for getting out of town. I stayed home in my room on weekends, reading books and daydreaming about being anywhere but Iowa. Ingrid and all the kids I'd been hanging out with had started pursuing harder drugs and I couldn't quite go there. I might go over to a girlfriend's house and watch a movie, but I avoided parties. I was tired of the crude jokes and the redneck guys I had hung out with as a freshman. All around me madness seemed to reign, and the Movement was getting crazier and crazier. A large wall was being built along the southern end of the campus, and I kept hearing about more and more friends of my mom's who were getting kicked out of the domes. I didn't want any of it to have anything to do with me and wanted to get far away from it all.

My dad encouraged me to take the college exams, then to come live with him in California and get residency so I could go to UC Santa Cruz. He'd gone there, and my grandfather had taught jazz there in the sixties, and he was sure with a good essay about growing up in a cult, I could get in. He thought they'd overlook my atrocious math scores and the notorious girl fight on my record if I wrote something heartfelt about growing up in a community where people could fly.

This idea of parlaying my experience into a stepping-stone confused me. For the last few years, I'd been slamming my head against the walls of my upbringing, trying to make the people around me see that they might be wrong. Everything felt so binary. You were a townie or you were a meditator. Maharishi was a living saint and we were living out his vision of Heaven on Earth, or he was a con man and we were fools. The idea that I didn't have to choose sides but instead could just walk away from this mess into another life seemed too good to be true. It also felt illicit to spill the secrets of our life inside the Movement. But if that was what it took to get out, I would do it.

As the ground was starting to thaw and Iowa slipped into mud season, I got a call from Ingrid wanting to know if I'd come to a party at Nick's house. I hadn't heard her voice in so long—she sounded tense and distracted. We agreed that I'd come over to her place and then—since neither of us had a car—Jiten would pick us up from there. I longed to connect with my friends again after a long winter of plotting my escape.

The stars seemed to be hanging especially low in the sky that night as I walked through the pathways of Utopia Park. The little poplar trees that were seedlings when I had moved in nearly a decade ago towered over the trailers. Their branches were bare of leaves, and the ground squished under my feet.

Walking through the corridors of mobile homes, I felt I'd outgrown this place. The trailer park had seemed so perfect when we moved in, but now I couldn't say "Utopia Park" without sneering to myself. The rusted metal, the grass overrun with weeds, the potholes and old cars—all the raggedy tackiness felt symbolic of how I'd come to see the community I was living in.

Ingrid's family lived in one of the hexagon-shaped buildings that had once housed the Parsons students. I pushed open the frosted glass doors and was blasted with the familiar warmth of their apartment. Ingrid's little sisters shrieked when they saw me—they raced to hug me and play with my hair. Ingrid was nowhere in sight; I tickled her sisters and made small talk with her parents, both re-served and erudite. Her father had always seemed intimidating to me, but tonight, they seemed warm and eager to talk. We discussed the new Sthapatya Vedic changes happening around campus. I told them I was thinking of moving away, that I wanted to attend col-lege, and they shushed their herd of children and nodded their heads with something that looked like relief.

When Ingrid came out of her room, I drew in my breath sharply. It had been about six weeks since I'd seen her—we were at dif-ferent schools—and she'd transformed. She had always been tall and slender, beautiful, with long shining hair and a delicate bone structure. But tonight she wore a pair of baggy jeans that hung off her waist. Even though it was eight o'clock at night, she wore sunglasses, and her skin looked taut and pale. She pushed past her parents, grabbing me by the arm and taking me out to the hallway to wait for Jiten, muttering something about being back in time for her curfew.

"You seem weird," I said to her. She laughed, and moved her sunglasses up so I could see her eyes.

"Whoa," I said. Her eyes were bloodshot, her eyelids heavy. Her face looked gaunt and aged—like some chain-smoking elderly bar-maid, not my gorgeous seventeen-year-old friend.

"Yeah, I've kind of gotten into meth a little." She laughed, as if it was just another wild lark for her—like stealing cheap wine or making out with townies.

When Jiten pulled up we climbed into his car, with me in the backseat, and he began telling us an almost impossible to believe story about Nick getting arrested by the Fairfield Police Depart-ment, and an ATF agent asking him to wear a wire during a drug deal. I felt so far away from everything as we drove through the slushy, muddy streets. My closest friends had gone down a rabbit hole that seemed to me every bit as illogical as the one we had gone down with Maharishi.

We walked into Nick's apartment, which was thick with smoke and filled with guys in puffy jackets. Nick's drug network had expanded throughout southeast Iowa. We found the pile of plastic cups and poured ourselves generous portions of vodka. Ingrid motioned for me to follow her to Nick's bedroom, where he and a few other guys were bent over a table, slicing up white lines of powder. They laughed with delight when they saw me—I had been hidden for months. Ingrid and Nick started chanting for me to do a line with them. I looked around the room of excited faces and decided nothing really mattered. I took the dollar bill handed to me, like I'd been doing it for ages, and quickly inhaled two lines.

My nostrils burned, as if someone had punched me in the head—only this being punched in the head felt kind of amazing. The door opened and Jackie walked in. I'd avoided her since we both had gotten kicked out of school. She leaned over and kissed Nick and then turned to me and gave me a shy smile. I smiled too—my whole body radiating warmth toward her as she bent down, moved her hair out of the way, and did three lines. Before I knew it, we were sitting in each other's laps in an easy chair, cuddling with each other and apologizing for everything that had gone wrong between us. The night passed in a blur as I watched more and more strangers pile into the apartment. I stayed with Jackie, nestled in the safety of our newly healed friendship. Around midnight, I got a ride home from a townie guy, who leaned in for a kiss. I slipped out of his truck before he could touch me, scampered past the gates of Utopia Park, and went into my trailer.

*   *   *

The next morning, I asked my mom to go for a walk. Bundled up in our jackets, we tromped through the mud on a path by the reservoir. We hadn't done much together lately, and I felt oddly nervous with her. We'd been living in close quarters but our private lives—my rebellion, her new spiritual focus—had created a chasm between us. I felt my heart hammering as our boots squished in the mud, through the tall grasses, the water of the reservoir glimmering in the morning sun.

Avoiding her eyes, I suddenly declared: "Mom, I want to move to California to live with Dad."

"What!" she said, staring at me. "No, you can't. No." I could hear the disbelief in her voice. I had been so caught up in my head, thinking about how to escape, I hadn't thought about how it would make her feel. I figured she knew I was going to college, and that she was preparing for me to leave anyway. But I hadn't thought about her feeling that I was choosing Dad over her.

Now, as her eyes welled up with tears, I realized how awful a betrayal this must have felt to her. "Why?" she asked, her voice breaking. But her mouth was already hardening into anger, her cheeks flushed with red.

I felt bereft. I wanted her to want this for me. I spoke quickly, telling her I had to leave, that things had gotten too dark for me here, that my friends were partying too hard, that I didn't fit in at the town school either, that I was tired of being an outcast in my hometown.

"But your dad isn't really an adult, Claire. And I have full custody."

I explained that it was a precollege scheme to get in-state tuition in California and save money. I hoped the financial reality of it would make her take it seriously. But she turned back on the path, and marched away from me, her shoulders hunched up and trembling. I knew my mom had been working nonstop for years to take care of me, while also changing the world. And here I was walking away from those choices, and choosing the parent who had done nothing but indulge his weaknesses. I felt overwhelmingly sad. But I still needed to get away, immediately.

PART THREE

Searching

CHAPTER SIXTEEN

Adulthood

I had an awful dream. In it, I raced through the dark maze of hallways of the Maharishi School of the Age of Enlightenment, a small band of pastel-suited school administrators chasing me. I ducked into a classroom, and in the moonlight I looked up to see a portrait of Maharishi staring down at me with clownlike beatitude. I pressed myself against the wall—as if the portrait could see me—and peered out the window wondering how I would escape.

Then I was outside, walking by a small creek lined with pussy willows and snake grass. Something was moving in the smoky darkness of the water. I looked more closely. In the shallows, a velveteen ball took form, cresting out of the water. I felt a horrible dawning, a sense of total recognition and understanding. A dark velvet submarine was rising—an absurd, silly-looking thing. At that moment, I knew that Maharishi had given his most demanding restriction yet to the meditators in Fairfield—that we must all live under the water. The devoted had obeyed. I now saw that the creek was filled with these velvet submarines, operated by desperate people trying to find water in our dry corner of the Midwest. *Sexy Sadie what have you done?* the Beatles had sung. *You made a fool of everyone.* Why had it taken me so long to understand?

I awoke in my bed, covered with sweat. It was 2004. I was twenty-seven years old, and by a combination of blind luck and dogged perseverance, I had landed an internship and freelance reporting gig at the *New York Times*. I was about to graduate from the Columbia Graduate School of Journalism. I had a booming social life and a future that looked hopeful. Thanks to my mom and the Maharishi School, I had a wonderful sense of destiny. Greatness awaited me—that had been hardwired into my brain. Even if I didn't believe in the overall vision that said I was a Brahmin reincarnated, deputized by Maharishi and the great wheel of karma to usher in the Age of Enlightenment, I still had the sense that I was chosen. Which was helpful from a morale point of view.

Not that I wasn't a hard worker—after all, I'd spent my childhood watching my mom hustle in and out the door as she juggled a multitude of jobs to get by. I had been financially independent since I moved out of my dad's apartment in Los Angeles in 1995 and headed to college at UC Santa Cruz, thanks to a bundle of student loans and other financial aid to get me through. Since then, I'd worked as a salesperson in an Iowa futon shop, a transcriptionist in Santa Cruz to a Russian economist, a marijuana harvester in Switzerland, a waitress in Paris, and an office assistant in a Santa Barbara software firm.

For the last few years—before I got the job at the *Times* and before I went to journalism school—I'd been working on Madison Avenue for a French luxury shampoo company, where I'd worked my way up to marketing manager. (No one else was actually in the marketing department, so it was a dubious title.) Still, in its way, my job was a delight. I'd flown to France and toured the factories where great vats of expensive creams were being mixed and boiled, and I'd sat in corporate boardrooms in the Midwest, hashing out the release of the latest in anti-frizz technology. The company was small and looked favorably on two-hour champagne lunches a few times a week. I had enough money to pay the rent for my one-bedroom Brooklyn apartment, slowly pay off my student loans, and buy myself ironic secretarial blouses and pencil skirts. In some ways, it was the fulfillment of my prepubescent fantasy of living in Manhattan. An office job that didn't require a lot of work but demanded nice clothes, and nights and weekends chockablock with parties and other events.

In those years, Maharishi and my life as a 'ru kid in Fairfield felt very far away. I meditated sporadically—when I was sick or wanted an excuse to be alone, or most reliably, during turbulent plane rides. But I was not on the Program. Not long after I'd moved away, my mom had moved out of Utopia Park and in with her boyfriend Ed. When I went back to visit her once or twice a year, I didn't go anywhere near the campus. Instead, I chose to curl up on my mom's couch and feast on the parade of homemade vegetarian treats and baked goods she made for me. Her move off campus and her new relationship seemed to have opened her up, made her more relaxed and happy. During the holidays, I would meet up with my other Maharishi School friends and we would get a thrill by going out late to the local townie bars, playing pool with rednecks, eating pickled eggs and blasting Def Leppard on the slimy jukebox. Now that I lived far away, with a life of my own, it felt more fun to pretend I was really an Iowan and not the outsider trapped between two worlds I'd felt like when I lived there.

But then, in 2001, Maharishi resurfaced. Less than two weeks after the 9/11 attacks, I opened the Sunday *New York Times* and saw a full-page ad placed by Maharishi. "Maharishi's Proposal for Permanent World Peace" read the headline, over a picture of "His Holiness Maharishi Mahesh Yogi." I felt a rising sense of hot shame, as if my drunk dad was yelling during a ceremony.

"When the U.S. government, with the most powerful defense force in the world, and a defense budget of over $300 billion, has hopelessly failed to defend its nation against the attacks of the enemy, what hope is there for any nation to protect itself against its enemies through the use of arms?" Maharishi asked.

He of course had the answer. He was setting up a $1 billion endowment fund, which would pay for forty thousand young men from "Vedic Families in India" to meditate all the time, generating "the Maharishi Effect," thus, once again, creating World Peace.

"There must be a few peace-loving billionaires in America who would understand our offer and who can immediately, in one day, create the required endowment fund to try this new peaceful angle of approach to establish permanent World Peace," Maharishi pleaded in fine print. "Due to the urgency of the situation it is being suggested that if someone is in a position to advance, rather than donate, one billion dollars, this advance will enable us to start the program immediately, and we will return this advance from the donations that are expected to follow."

Even though I had grown up with Maharishi weaving himself into world events, this felt somehow shocking. This was my world, the real world, and yet here he was still suggesting that money and meditation were the answer. Beyond the absurdity of it, the events of that day were too real for me to feel dismissive—my brother had watched both planes fly into the buildings, and had run away as they fell on the streets behind him. I had spent the day safely in Midtown, desperate to hear from him. In the days and weeks to come, living in New York felt like being inside a throbbing wound. I walked to work every day past handmade flyers of missing loved ones. In the evenings, I would sit with my brother on his rooftop in Brooklyn and his voice would break as he described trying to shake the image of watching the bodies fall from the sky. So seeing this dippy proposal from Maharishi and his call for "peace-loving billionaires" made my blood boil.

For me, this was the beginning of the final chapter of Maharishi's life. In the months and years after 9/11, his outlandish demands for money grew louder and more insistent. The following year, he gave his first televised interview in twenty-five years to Larry King, who had once been a meditator. It was hard to watch—Maharishi had aged so much since he was the plump-faced gnome that I'd watched on the telecast as a kid. He had lost much of his hair, and what was left hung in gray wisps on the side of his hardened face. He seemed less joyous and more angry.

He called democracy a failure and he said he was starting his own government. In Fairfield, this shift meant even more Vedic projects. In 2003, Maharishi had expanded further on his outlandish business venture: for-profit "Peace Palaces." As part of his plan to rebuild the world according to his branded "Maharishi Sthapatya Vedic Architecture," these twelve-thousand-square-foot structures would house large groups of young Indian men who would chant from ancient Indian texts. In doing so, they would, of course, create World Peace.

"People do different things to earn money," said Maharishi, sitting in his usual cross-legged position for a televised press conference from his ashram in Holland. "They go into a profession or a business—they even go into the military and kill people as long as they get money. So why can't creating peace be a profession that makes money? Building Peace Palaces is a way to do something good that will promote happy, healthy individuals and a peaceful world—and earn money."

Maharishi announced that several of the palaces had already been built, including one in Maharishi Vedic City, Iowa, population ninety-nine, just a few miles outside Fairfield. But that summer there was little evidence of any such structure. A yellow flag with a red sunburst—the flag of Vedic City—waved in the wind above the gravel country road leading into the tiny town. Iowa's newest city had been officially incorporated in 2001—but for nearly a decade before, a group of developers working for Maharishi had been quietly buying the land from unsuspecting locals. The city, surrounded by farms, had then been laid out on a grid that corresponded to key astrological bodies, and each house was built according to Maharishi's somewhat random architectural specifications, which required, among other things, an eastward orientation, a center atrium, and detached garages.

A few dozen brightly colored houses formed the circular core of the town. In addition to these homes, Vedic City housed The Raj—a resort hotel and spa—as well as an observatory, an organic sunflower farm, an all-girls elementary school, and a town hall where the mayor lived. But that summer, despite the guru's excited promises, no Peace Palace emerged.

On campus, I heard through my mother and her friends that access to the dome was becoming more restrictive. My mom, who had been going to the dome sporadically in recent years, went less and less. She meditated alone in her bedroom, on the other side of town. It seemed in some ways she too was becoming more Iowan and less guru.

When I was a kid, Fairfield had been a ghost town in the afternoons during Program time, because going to the dome had been a nonnegotiable part of life. But now, on my visits back, I would run into my mother's friends at the video store or the grocery store. To see people out at six o'clock made it feel like a regular Midwestern town, the meditators, like my mom, inadvertent Iowans. It made me uncomfortable—like seeing your parents naked. They would act strangely guilty about it—explaining from out of nowhere that they had started meditating at home, or that they had in fact been kicked out of the dome. Many seemed untethered, lost.

The look of Fairfield had changed too. In the years since I'd moved away, Maharishi and his administration had demolished half a dozen historical buildings because they were made of stone—and Maharishi had come to believe the stone gave off bad spiritual radiation. Two ponds and a grove of willow trees at the center of the campus had been drained and bulldozed to avoid the same spiritual radiation. A marshy field remained, with a wooden bridge rising out of the grass, waterlogged and worn, decorated with bronze globes. The division between what Maharishi envisioned and what was real had expanded. The campus looked like the home of a schizophrenic, Indian émigré billionaire. Brochures were available in local shops, showing carefully drawn models of cities like New York, retrofitted to suit Maharishi's notion of world peace. I gawked at the before and after images of Paris. The gorgeous, circular arrangement of Baron Haussmann's design had been redone into a pastel-colored grid, with little golden castles at key intersections. I tried to imagine Maharishi's grasp of reality—not to mention his followers'—if they thought the French would bulldoze the Eiffel Tower and replace it with a golden yellow office tower to house a library of Maharishi's writings.

Meanwhile, Maharishi had crowned a Lebanese scientist, Tony Nader, king, or more specifically "His Majesty Maharaja Adhiraj Raja Raam." Together, they went about the business of founding the Global Country of World Peace. Maharishi tried to find a piece of land where he could have national sovereignty. He bought several islands, and according to local press reports got pretty far along in negotiations with the president of Suriname, offering him $1.3 billion dollars for a 200-year lease of more than 8,000 acres. In addition, he pledged 1 percent of the money the central bank put into circulation and the promise of creating thousands of jobs. Similar efforts to create a "Vatican-like sovereign city-state," as Maharishi once described it, were made in the island nation of Tuvalu, and on one of the Northern Mariana Islands. In Costa Rica, officials from the Global Country of World Peace offered each family on the Talamanca reservation $250 in exchange for the right to appoint a king. A ceremony was held, but when the security minister allegedly caught wind of it, he asked the representatives of the Global Country of World Peace to leave. Each time, the governments decided that Maharishi's vision was too far out for them. Just when I thought Maharishi had done the craziest thing he could possibly do, he'd do something crazier, even more nonsensical.

His imperious behavior had started to backfire. Earl Kaplan, who believes he was Maharishi's largest benefactor, had suddenly accused him of being a con artist and a thief. When I was growing up, Earl had been the guy who made tofu out of a shed on the wrong side of town. He wore plaid button-downs and white sneakers and was earnest and kind. He'd been on my mom's teacher-training course in Spain, and he always greeted us with warmth. His two kids had been just a few years behind me in school. But more than the personal connections, Earl seemed evangelical about sharing his story—he wanted people to understand what had happened to him.

On May 8, 1997, inside their office headquarters in Fairfield, Iowa, Earl and his twin brother, David, had opened a bottle of champagne. The brothers, who had grown up in a middle-class suburb of St. Louis, had just sold half of their company to *Reader's Digest* for $145 million. Earl had started the business less than a decade earlier, abandoning his tofu manufacturing to sell surplus books to local hospitals and elementary schools out of the dilapidated garage behind his house. With the help of his brother, Earl had slowly built his company, Books Are Fun, into a thriving empire.

The forty-seven-year-old brothers were light-headed, smiling and joking about their lives as newly rich men. "Let's call Maharishi!" said David.

After more than two decades of devout practice, they were certain that their guru, Maharishi Mahesh Yogi, was the one to thank for their incredible fortune. For the last few years, they had become very close to the reclusive and powerful guru, and they had been given the rare privilege of spending time with him in his remote ashram in Holland. Maharishi had treated them like princes, giving them countless hours of spiritual and economic guidance. In return, they had donated tens of millions of dollars of profits from their thriving business.

Even before the deal with *Reader's Digest*, the brothers had arranged to give Maharishi and his organization $35 million from the proceeds, with the agreement that most of the money would be used to pay part of the debt incurred for Heavenly Mountain, an opulent retreat the Kaplans and Maharishi's Movement had built outside Boone, North Carolina.

David dialed the secret number in the Netherlands, and a few minutes later they had the guru on the line. His Yoda-like voice on speakerphone, he offered a few words of congratulations. The brothers were grinning from ear to ear, their hearts filled with adoration. But then Maharishi added a caveat: "You don't mind if we use this money for something else, do you?"

Earl was a little surprised. Maharishi had been talking about paying off the mountain retreat debt for several years, and Earl had determinedly applied his business acumen to this cause. Maharishi promised Earl that the retreat would still be used for the groups of men and women who had dedicated their lives to celibate, full-time meditation. Now, he said the money was instead needed in India. Earl quickly checked his feelings. The Maharishi's knowledge was subtle, cosmic, and omniscient. There must be a good reason for this, he thought, because Maharishi knows best. But Maharishi wasn't finished.

"You know thirty-five million is really not that much money," the voice on the speakerphone crackled, filled with its usual mirth and wisdom. "Why don't you think about giving one hundred million?"

Two years later, in 1999, Earl sold the rest of his company to *Reader's Digest* for a total of $380 million. He was honored in the TM Movement as embodying Maharishi's formula of living 200 percent of life: 100 percent spiritual success and 100 percent material success. In recent years, Earl had given additional millions to Maharishi's various charity organizations. He had built a palatial home just north of Utopia Park. Bordered by iron gates and bronze lions, the house was an opulent vision, although it was just off a gravel road and next to a field of soybeans. The massive front doors were painted with golden lotus leaves, and the grounds were arranged in mazelike gardens, which ended in a fountain, a pool, and a water slide.

And then, overnight it seemed, Earl became an outspoken critic of Maharishi. He accused him of misappropriating the $35 million he had given him to create World Peace. Earl had become enraged after he'd discovered that the bank account set up specifically to finance the construction and maintenance of the spiritual center in North Carolina had been emptied.

Now, Earl was bringing a lawsuit against Maharishi's international organization, purported to be worth between $4 and $5 billion. After noting the distinct absence of World Peace, Earl extricated himself from the Movement and moved to a hilltop compound in Malibu. The Movement, in turn, disavowed him— as well as his brother David. The Movement claimed he was mentally unstable, pointing to his newfound interest in shamanic Judaism and his marriage to an aspiring model half his age.

At that point, I was working as an intern at the *New York Times*, and when I heard the rumors of Earl's defection, I wanted to figure out for myself what was going on. Despite comparing himself to Neo in *The Matrix*, Earl sounded fairly coherent to me when I called him. Earl told me that, after doing some research of his own, he was convinced that Maharishi had been nefarious from the start. He even said that Guru Dev's nephew was alleging that as a young student, Maharishi had murdered his master—Guru Dev—in a bid for power and money. Supposedly the nephew of the long-dead guru was accusing Maharishi of being a murderous, ambitious plotter who had stolen the sacred magic of India and commoditized it for the West.

After ending the interview, all I wanted to do was go home and meditate—but given what I'd heard, that didn't seem appropriate. I dutifully wrote out the transcript and saved it on my computer.

I didn't know what to do with that information or how dreadful it made me feel.

After the Columbia Graduate School of Journalism I went on to the University of Chicago Divinity School, convinced my destiny was to write about faith and religion and belief. But in the jobs that followed, I strayed a bit from that mission. At the *Los Angeles Times*, I'd reported some of the most godless beats on offer: the porn industry, talent agents, and the entertainment business. More and more, I seemed to be specializing in assholes, rather than religious movements or the mystical underworld.

When I quit the *Los Angeles Times* in 2007, I started working as a freelance magazine writer. I had more work than I'd ever had. I'd just gotten my first investigative assignment from *Rolling Stone* and was finishing up a months' long project on fundamentalist Mormons for *Portfolio.* Although I was at the relative beginning of my career, I was already far more successful than I had ever imagined I'd be—which at times was a little awkward to talk about with my mom and my brother. It was as if I had come down with some strange, benign disorder that everyone tried to respectfully ignore. Maybe it was the humble Midwestern aspect that had soaked into our family, or the spiritual focus of the TM Movement, but for some reason my ambition felt like something I had to hide.

Stacey had taken a very different approach to life and ambition. Instead of college, he'd traveled the world. Handsome, with a wry sense of humor, he taught himself photography. He stayed up late into the night, making electronic music. He would work just long enough to make the money he needed to go on his next excursion, and then he'd disappear for months at a time. That spring, he was between jobs, after having lived in Puerto Rico for a few years. He was on contract with an electrical engineering company in L.A. to set up high-end audio systems. He didn't love the work though he seemed to be good at it. He was meticulous and exacting when he chose to be, but in between jobs, he crashed. Hard.

So when he had recently called to ask if he could live with me in L.A. for a month, I hesitated. I knew he would put a damper on my work and social life. Stacey tended to be overly protective of me, telling me variously that I was working too hard, took things too seriously, that I was too anxious, too ambitious.

On the night that he arrived, he set up a Blu-ray DVD player in my living room—a gift!—and then took some Valium. Now, he was making his way through the entire *Planet Earth* BBC video series. For the third time.

Outside my window, the sun was setting, turning the hills of Silver Lake a pink-violet. I was sitting at my desk, with the sounds of *Planet Earth* playing behind me, when I noticed my phone was vibrating. I took it outside—I didn't want my brother to hear my all-business voice if it was work related. But it was a text message from a girl I knew from the Maharishi School. "The Rish has dropped his body."

I felt something electric and strange inside. In that moment, I realized there was some small part of me that never believed he would actually die.

Her wording reflected the view shared by most everyone in Fairfield—that when Maharishi died, he would simply shift from the human form to the magical enlightened, omniscient ether. Standing on my small deck, I took a moment to be alone with the knowledge that he was gone. For a moment, it felt like this was about just Maharishi and me. I had never met him, but he had entirely shaped my life. Some small part of me believed that he knew me, that he sensed me across the universe and that he understood the intimate, silent place TM had given me.

And yet for the previous decade, I'd felt an almost relentless contempt for him. It had been hard for me to talk about him or our Movement without my lips curling into a knowing sneer. I had never used the word "master" to describe Maharishi despite this being par for the course in the guru/devotee relationship.

The feeling I felt now was sort of like a slave unshackled, surprised to find an enormous sense of longing for her master.

I walked inside.

"Maharishi died," I said simply.

"Huh," Stacey grunted. Then he mumbled, "Guess he wasn't immortal after all," and continued to stare at the TV.

I felt heavy, almost like I couldn't move. I thought of all the people I was closest to in my life—my mom, my brother, my mother's ex-boyfriend Jeff, my high school friends: Jiten, Ingrid, Wells, Joey. All these people I treasured had been brought together by this faraway man. And now he was gone. Knowing that he'd left the world, I felt his loss as you would a loved one.

I turned back to my computer and saw that my in-box was filling up. My mom: "We are hearing here that Maharishi is dead." The *Los Angeles Times* obituary editor: "How do we reach his press people?" And a forwarded e-mail from someone in the Movement with an official announcement from Maharaja Adhiraj Raja Raam, aka Tony Nader, his words in a golden font:

Jai Guru Dev.

Everyone has applauded. It is heaven that is now applauding—

for heaven is the happiest of us. It has just welcomed and opened its arms to His Holiness Maharishi Mahesh Yogi.

It's a very difficult announcement to make to all of you, but this is his wish and his will. And he decided to achieve it and make it in great peace with all of you assembled, and all of us together. And all the heavens and the Devetas applauding, and opening their arms, and rejoicing—for he has gone to them yet he still is with us—him being everything, totality and wholeness.

We have many many reasons to be troubled and sad and to cry if we want, but the reality is, we have also to accept his wish, and to bow down to the will of heaven for a work beautifully done. A transformation of humanity never seen in any time for any generation, in any Yuga.

Together we will be strong, unified, uphold his teaching, and keep being honoured [*sic*] for having had the chance to have a glimpse of him, or hear a word from him.

Today is a very special day that he must have selected. We respect that. We maintain our dignity and his message in our minds and hearts and the purity of his teaching, and the purity of our intentions and the unity of [ourselves]—for only together, strong and unified, we can have the sense of fulfilling his presence continuing on this planet earth.

Stacey had fallen asleep on the couch, and was softly snoring. I felt alone and a pang of longing to be with others. Two girlfriends from Fairfield were planning on making their way to Varanasi where a huge funeral was being planned. I felt a sting of envy—a familiar one—because I was being left out of the celebration. I looked at my meager savings account, already earmarked for student loan payments, and felt torn. The trip to Varanasi, as with all things Maharishi, was prohibitively expensive.

A few days later, Stacey and I tuned in to the online Maharishi Channel late in the evening to watch the funeral on the other side of the world. Maharishi's lifeless body had been flown to India, propped up for days in a seated meditation pose, his eyes closed peacefully, as if in a momentary state of reflection. He was given full state honors for his funeral in Allahabad.

The funeral scene by the Ganges felt alienating. They had draped Maharishi's dead body in extravagant robes. His body was cremated and the ashes scattered over the river, accompanied by a seemingly endless throng of followers. They placed them on a flower-laden funeral pyre, pushed it out into the sacred waters. People wept, sang, chanted, held each other. The live feed crackled. When they came into focus, the images were bizarre. There were a fair number of Western followers there, some of them wearing white robes and golden crowns. These were his Rajas, his newly anointed council of global leaders for the Movement he had left behind. Seeing them in action, in their tacky costumes and engaged in their ritualistic behavior, was off-putting. I had a sense that I had been part of something ancient and spiritual and beautiful. Yet the white men in golden crowns were a cutting reminder of how cultish Maharishi's Movement had become. Maharishi presented the same conundrum in death as he had in life: that which felt sublime and comforting was always laced with the bizarre and questionable.

CHAPTER SEVENTEEN

A New Utopia

Only a few weeks after Maharishi's death, I drove my car up the winding curves of Benedict Canyon, inhaling the sweet springtime smell of night jasmine. I felt off-kilter and nervous. At a friend's prodding, a young entrepreneur named Ben Goldhirsh had called to invite me on a date. I knew who he was even before that phone call. He had been the subject of a front-page magazine story in the *Los Angeles Times* the year before. "Can This 26-year-old Save the World?" the headline read. Ben had started a magazine called *GOOD*, aimed at people who believed in making positive change in the world. Both his parents had died when he was young and had left him with a substantial inheritance and a foundation. He was the poster child of youthful idealism. When I'd seen the article about him, I'd felt both self-contempt and cynicism. At twenty-nine, I had never even considered trying to save the world—only myself.

But Ben had sounded so casual and relaxed about our date on the phone, telling me to just come over to his house and we'd figure it out from there. He added enthusiastically that I could meet his dog. I was struck by his simplicity and ease in setting this up.

He lived at the end of a long, winding, crumbly road. When

I passed through the open gates to his house, I was surprised by the total darkness—it was like being in the backwoods of Iowa—something you didn't typically experience in Los Angeles. I felt a flash of nostalgia—for Iowa, for the silence.

I parked at the base of a hill, next to a small ranch house with all the lights out. I opened the car door, and above me, I heard a voice shout from the hill.

"Hello?"

"Hi!" I said, feeling a little like Dorothy in Oz.

"I hope you're cool with dogs," the voice shouted. If I hadn't been, it would've been too late—in the darkness, I could make out a massive animal barreling toward me down the hill. I steeled myself. Daryl, the size of a small horse, slammed his body into my crotch at top speed. Ben was walking down the steep driveway after him, his figure compact and muscular in the shadows.

"Hi," I said. "It's really dark."

Ben laughed, walked right up to me, staring into my eyes, and gave me a huge warm bear hug. Something about him—and the hug—the smell of his body, the scratchy feel of his beard, seemed deeply protective and familiar.

We walked up into his house and he offered me a tour. It was a strange place for a twenty-seven-year-old man—extremely tasteful and well decorated in a rustic sort of cowboy way. Layered on top of that, however, were dirty dishes, beer bottles, and clothes in small piles everywhere. I couldn't help but think that he cared very little about this date—why else would he leave his underwear on the floor?

He poured us whiskey and we went out to his porch. There was no sign or mention of dinner. We sat down and he started asking me about my religion blog. I had been writing for *The Washing-*

ton Post's religion Web site for the last year. He seemed genuinely interested in the topic; he mentioned that his sister had become more religious after his parents died. We argued a little about faith, but it felt playful, definitely not threatening. *He's smart*, I thought. *Nice eyes. Nice guy.* He seemed to be impressed by my graduate degrees. Sensing his "I-was-a-president-of-my-boarding-school" confidence, I started regaling him with stories of Iowa. I felt some misguided desire to show him how tough I was. So I recounted for him not the Maharishi/meditator Iowa but the rural Iowa of pig farms and methamphetamine. He egged me on to tell him stories of high school—bar fights, acid trips, meth parties. At midnight, he announced that he was tired. I got up from the porch chair, and we exchanged a slightly awkward hug and I fled, embarrassed to have been prattling on about all this seedy stuff to a guy who was supposedly changing the world. I felt that familiar pang from high school—I wasn't quite nice enough for the good kids. Still, I went to bed with a funny sort of sweet feeling. It was subtle and sweet—not physical or boozy. I hadn't had a date like that ever before.

In the months and years that followed, I confronted Maharishi's death in the only way I knew how—as a journalist. I did an interview with David Lynch for my blog at the *Washington Post*; the filmmaker had been touring the country talking about how great TM was for making you creative and happy. He'd even written a book about meditation and creativity called *Catching the Big Fish*.

That day after Maharishi died, he almost wept on the phone talking about Maharishi's death and, again, I felt pushed away. Even as I felt his loss and the enormous impact he'd had on my life, I didn't love Maharishi. In the end, despite years of exposure to his words, his photographs, his lectures and videotapes and edicts, his dreams and his ambitions, Maharishi was still a stranger to me.

I also interviewed Deepak Chopra, who as a kid had once been considered heir apparent to Maharishi until they had a falling out. I asked him the question that had always nagged me: Was Maharishi really an omniscient enlightened being who was trying to push the world to peace? Or was he a man, an imperfect and absurd man?

"I could never decide," Chopra told me over the phone, his voice dipping down with sadness. "He had a big ego. But maybe he genuinely thought of himself that way. People would talk about Buddha or Jesus, and he would dismiss it. He thought he was the real thing and these other guys, they weren't."

We talked about the 1980s and 1990s, and the astronomical rise in the cost of meditation training. "I used to resent that," Chopra said. "I think it's not fair to have a caste system. My guess was that he was being practical but I also felt that there could've been room for scholarships and other means of helping people. There was not enough charity, and if there was it was always directed to India."

"Maharishi was in a certain state of consciousness," Chopra told me. "He's very archetypal in a way. He was living out his archetypal energies but he was so powerful that these other people were living in it. There's a thin line between psychosis and genius, and it's like the razor's edge here."

A few years later, it was Lynch who had become the de facto face of the Transcendental Meditation Movement. Before Maharishi's death, in 2005, John Hagelin and Bobby Roth, who spent decades as leaders in Maharishi's Movement, suggested that Lynch start a foundation dedicated to helping troubled children through meditation. Lynch quickly expanded on the idea: he wanted to raise

$7 billion to spread TM. He wrote a book, *Catching the Big Fish: Meditation, Consciousness, and Creativity*, and he toured the world, speaking to young people about how fundamental meditation was to his artistic process.

Following Maharishi's death, Lynch, with lots of help from Bobby Roth, seemed to be quietly rebranding TM. He never mentioned Fairfield, he rarely mentioned Maharishi or the flying technique. He focused entirely on the practice as a simple technique for stress relief that—he told anyone who would listen—could transform a person's life.

One morning, Lynch invited me over to his house to participate in a group meditation and to interview him for a few minutes afterward for the *New York Times* magazine. The event was small but packed with twenty-something TV stars and musicians who had recently learned TM through Lynch's foundation. When I told a few of them that I had grown up meditating and studied at the Maharishi School, I found myself surrounded as they all wanted to know what it was like. "That's the dream," one guy kept saying over and over. I felt odd—when had TM become this cool shiny thing that great-looking successful young people were a part of? And who was I to deny the value of TM to people who needed it?

After the meditation, I tromped up the hill with Lynch to his painting studio where he said he would answer a few more of my questions. I was asking him about his convictions about his experiences of deeper levels of consciousness when I felt him start to give me a sharp look. He sounded defensive as he leaned toward me. "You can't imagine yourself to bliss. When you feel it and when you kick in there it's real." He watched as I scribbled down his answers and then he stared at me. He knew that I'd been a student at the Maharishi School, that I'd been meditating for a long time, and that I'd gone on the flying course. But during the process of writing the story, he seemed nervous about my curiosity concerning his belief and passion for Maharishi's cause. "Now, Claire. Let me ask you a question if I could. When I first met you, when we were going in the car, I felt, okay, Claire's been meditating for thirty-two years, but I felt that you had doubts. Is that a real feeling?"

I felt my cheeks grow red, and weirdly, I felt something like sadness and shame. Like in the old days when I knew that I wasn't ideal. "I think I'm an extremely doubtful person," I said quietly.

"What do you doubt about your meditation?" he asked. I paused—I had no doubts about my meditation. But, I told him, my experience was different from his—I'd dealt with an institutionalized TM that he'd never had to deal with.

"I know what you mean, but you feel you rebelled against that big time?" he asked in his squeaky Midwestern voice. "I still meditate," I told him carefully. "But to answer your question, I think doubting may be a character thing, you know? It may just be who I am."

"No," he said firmly. "I don't think so because I think people have doubts on the path, and then you need to get answers, and then once you get an answer, boom, you're set, you're going again, you know what I mean?"

I told him I thought I might just be a person who always would be doubtful. I delivered this fact with a trembling voice, wistful that I wouldn't get to believe in all the amazing things Lynch did. "It must be nice to be sure," I told him. "And maybe I'm jealous that you're sure?" I said carefully. This emotionally personal back-and-forth was unchartered waters for me as a journalist.

"I'll tell you what gets me a lot of times. Maharishi has said some strange things along the road, like 'damn the democracy.' You first hear this and you say this is just crazy." I watched Lynch carefully now, nodding my head. I knew Maharishi had called for a monarchy but did Lynch really back this up? Where could he be going? And could I print this? "And then you hear this phrase, 'united we stand, divided we fall.' We got the divided states of America. It's a trick. We're divided almost down the middle. And in this, democracy is a strange thing that we embrace like crazy, but it can be used in bad ways. And I think people are seeing that these days, so I started thinking whoa, I get that."

We were both quiet as we looked at each other. He had a big smile on his face and was waiting for me to affirm what he'd said. That our democracy had failed? That Maharishi was actually right about everything?

I gave him a tight smile and said quietly, "I wish I had that." And I wasn't kidding. I wished I could believe like that. But I couldn't.

It's an odd idea—having doubts about meditation. Reams of scientific studies have shown that meditation in general and Transcendental Meditation in particular can give practitioners enormous health benefits. TM has been shown to lower your heart rate; lower your cholesterol level; lower incidents of heart attack, hypertension, and obesity. Scientific studies have shown that TM is helpful in losing weight, quitting smoking, helping with attention deficit disorders as well as depression. Dr. Norman Rosenthal, a respected researcher and psychologist who helped discover seasonal affective disorder, wrote a book in 2011 called *Transcendence*, which argues that TM is the solution to an overstressed, depressed world. If you visit tm.org, Dr. Mehmet Oz will greet you via a video testimonial, telling you about how in the three years since he's learned TM, his life has changed. Even the government has joined the masses, with the VA commissioning a government-funded program in several of their hospitals that uses TM to help veterans returning from the wars in Iraq and Afghanistan alleviate posttraumatic stress disorder.

The TM that David Lynch presented to the world was the TM that I myself believed in—a simple practice that felt really good. I loved that he drank coffee before he meditated and enjoyed a cigarette afterward. It felt irreverent and nonconformist and cool. But when we were away from the crowd, it felt like Lynch wanted to make sure I believed that Maharishi's way was the Truth, that he hadn't been a man who had made mistakes or had his own selfish impulses. I couldn't go back there.

CHAPTER EIGHTEEN

The Flying Course

When I married Ben, I felt many things—joy, excitement, head-over-heels adoration—all those newlywed feelings I'd hoped for but never imagined would be mine. And I felt an enormous sense of relief. I had somehow managed to emerge from my long-standing emotional fortress and find a big-hearted, handsome guy who said he would love me forever. But it was also a hard transition. I had been used to being my own person for a very long time. I'd succeeded by keeping a close lookout for myself. No one was ever going to take advantage of me or hurt me, because I was on constant patrol. Now, in order to make marriage work, I needed to be open to somebody in a way that I hadn't allowed.

Meanwhile, parenthood ended up coming hand and hand with our marriage—I found out that I was pregnant two days before our wedding.

When Josie was born, I was overwhelmed by my daughter's beauty and innocence and, in the same instant, absolutely terrified of taking it away, of hurting her in any way. Even though it wasn't necessary financially, I went back to work almost immediately. I had become an assistant professor at UC Riverside two years before (just a few miles from where my parents met and fell in love on a

TM retreat); I taught journalism and creative writing. The terrible truth is that after I had my daughter, I had started to hate my job. But I also didn't like the fact that suddenly friends and strangers alike had started calling me "Mom." I clung to the professorship long after it had served me.

When I'd return home exhausted after a long day of commuting and teaching, I couldn't help but think of my own mom. It was hard for me to feel too sorry for myself when the truth was, I had an enviable, well-paid job. And moreover, I didn't even actually need to work. We had enough money for me to stay at home and stare at my baby all day if I'd chosen that. But I couldn't allow myself to enjoy this financial security. Instead I used it as a tool in my head to undermine myself. Internal monologues that began with self-pity—I'm so tired, I hate my job—immediately turned into a sense of self-contempt. How dare I be unhappy when I had a beautiful baby, a loving husband, a big house, and everything I needed financially?

And yet I *was* unhappy. I thought of my mom constantly. Suddenly her choice to move us to rural Iowa to join a group of people who were meditating and hoping to change the world seemed admirable and inspiring. It felt like the opposite of my life juggling obligations and conforming to some vague idea of what successful and normal looked like. I had become keenly aware of the aura of magic and hope that had surrounded my early years. I thought of the constant celebrations and goals that checkered my childhood and I found myself nostalgic. It had felt so important. Without meditation and Maharishi's mission, did I have a way to engage with life in a meaningful way? A way to raise a kid?

About a year after Josie was born, Ben had come home from work and collapsed on the sofa. Our dogs were barking to be fed. Upstairs, our daughter was screaming in her crib. I had just put her down to sleep for the night, and I looked anxiously back toward her room, then turned to Ben, hoping he would volunteer to go soothe her. He got up from the couch and fed the dogs as he complained about work. Then he pulled out a box of frozen chicken tenders from the freezer and popped them into the microwave. That would be our dinner. As the timer beeped away the seconds, I heard Josie's sobs slowing and fading as she found her own way to soothe herself to sleep.

I poured myself a glass of white wine. Ben pulled out hot sauce from the fridge. "How was your day?" he asked, distracted. I half-heartedly began to recite a story about how a phone interview I'd done had gotten weird, but he wasn't really listening. The microwave trilled. Ben grabbed his chicken tenders and made a beeline for the couch, leaving me in midsentence.

I'd been holed up in the house all day, tacking between nursing Josie and grading papers for the class I taught. I was eager for human contact, some reminder that I was still the interesting and sane person I'd been before becoming a mom. *So this is it?* asked a quiet voice in my head. *Is this what your life is now?* Microwaved chicken tenders and a crying baby and a husband who needs you to disappear so he can get some peace and quiet?

I left the room, unnoticed, and trudged up the long stairway to our bedroom. I got in our bed and sat up against the pillows and stared into the middle distance. All the stuff around me—the bed, the furniture, the shoe collection—all the carefully curated elements of my life were closing in, weighing me down.

I was scared of how I felt. And I was scared of hurting my marriage, or worse, my daughter. But there was a part of me that wanted to run away, back to Iowa. I kept thinking about what it had been like to be a kid in a utopian community, always caught up in some global plan to change the world, all our actions supercharged with meaning. We meditators felt as if we were part of something important. With basic economic anxieties at bay, I started to wrestle with the big questions: Beyond mere survival, what was the point of living? Was the feeling of transcendence I had known as a child something I could still invite into my life? As a cynic and a skeptic, could I ever have a divine experience? Could I let go of my rationality long enough to experience something other? Something like what my mother and our community back in Fairfield had created?

I wanted to believe in believing again.

It was that longing, in the end, that sent me back to my hometown that summer. That night, with the sound of the microwave trilling and ESPN blasting, I decided to call the TM Center in Fairfield and sign up for the Flying Course. As I walked into a dim basement, my eyes adjusting to the darkness, I squinted, looking for my spot. I had set myself up close to the door because I wanted to be able to get out quickly if necessary. I found my pillows and blankets and sat down, arranging them just so. The entire room was covered from wall to wall in old mattress foam, the familiar rectangles draped in saggy white sheets. On the walls, two hand-painted banners hung, and in careful gold and green cursive, they read, "Yogic Flying Competition."

The experience of returning to the TM world of my youth was strange in ways I hadn't expected. I was listening to tapes of Maharishi in buildings I hadn't been inside for decades. The buildings that had been spared the Sthapatya Vedic razing of the nineties were untouched, like mausoleums to my youth.

That sense of being frozen in time extended to some of the people I saw. I gasped during one of our nightly meals in the dining hall when I saw Dr. Rowe, the school administrator from when I was a kid. His hair had gone from black to gray but otherwise his face was unchanged, waxen and without a wrinkle. I saw so many familiar faces like this—staff and administration and faculty who had remained at the university for a lifetime, working doggedly at enacting Maharishi's vision.

It was as if time had stopped. None of them had built much of a life for themselves outside this campus; instead of retirement accounts they were still giving whatever extra money they had to Maharishi's programs. But their faces looked younger than the baby boomers I knew in California. Perhaps they had been preserved by some potent and ineffable mix of meditation and unyielding belief.

Our group had started out with twenty women, but now we were down to eight, the attrition based on achievement. Once you attained "flight," you got to leave the group to go meditate alone. I felt bad for these other women who were left—I imagined they were surprised by their failure. But I had expected it. And yet there I was, sitting in that room, eyes closed, waiting to repeat my mantra and levitate.

The bell rang and all the murmuring and whispering stopped. Every once in a while there was a flicker of lightning and a rumble of thunder from a late-afternoon storm. Inside the dim room, the old air conditioner rattled at full tilt. "Believe," I implored myself. "You have to try."

Sitting in a basement on a floor covered in foam, I realized that maybe I just wasn't meant to be happy, or to fly. I wanted to be wrong. I wanted my own eye-rolling response to be wrong. I wanted the idea of faith and meaning to not be a socially constructed illusion as I had learned to view them in divinity school, nor a masterful fraud by a malevolent con man, but an accessible worldview. After all I'd been through, I wanted some version of the Utopia to be real.

Our teacher, Linda, sat in the corner, the very picture of a matronly, bohemian rhapsody in her fire-orange sari, her eyes closed, her straight, graying hair parted down the middle, clamped tight with sparkly barrettes. She swayed gently, eyes shut, as if something had hold of her. I felt envious.

"All riiiiight, my little chickadees," she said in her singsong voice. "I think today some of you are going to hatch."

Some girls laughed at the joke, even though she'd been saying this for days now. When I felt her eyes pass over me, twinkling and merry, I quickly attempted a happy look. I didn't want her to know I was thinking my usual stream of negative thoughts—Maharishi was a con artist, this was a trick, all these people were faking it.

"Now remember what Maharishi says," she went on. "No one is going to come along and give you a cosmic broom. You just have to fly!" With that she rang the big brass bell she kept at her side— next to a picture of the guru—signaling the beginning of afternoon meditation. I closed my eyes.

"Believe," I implored myself.

Anything would do. It didn't matter, even if it was a tiny gesture or odd, I just wanted something different to take place. Some slight detour from the status quo of being me. My whole body tingled with electric anticipation. I was hyperconscious of every sensation in my body as I tried to repeat my new mantra with focus and intention. Everything leads up to this moment, I thought. One way or another, I'll know the truth. I'll know whether I can change who I am.

I said the mantra and waited. Then I felt a sort of warmth and a strange intensity. "You're just imagining that," I thought as a rush of energy quivered down my spine.

After little bursts of heavy breathing and a few giggles died down, a hushed silence settled in. Fifteen minutes later, Linda rang her little golden bell. I felt a strange sense of relief. Nothing had happened to me, but nothing had happened to anyone else either. We rested for an allotted ten minutes, our bodies on the soft communal bed, and suddenly I felt a gentle sort of camaraderie with these women. Maybe I wasn't so different from them.

It was later, when we tried again, that I finally "flew." It was silent. I'd been meditating for hours alone in my room already that day. I wanted it more than anything now—some sense of shift. Now, when it came time to say the flying mantra, I rocked my body a little and felt the mantra taking over. I decided to just "let" my body bounce. What happened next is, for me, beyond coherent explanation: My brain went totally silent, and I felt like I almost blacked out. For an instant I feel as if I was somewhere otherworldly, somewhere beautiful. It was the same deep darkness that I'd gotten to during my best meditations. But bigger. For a brief moment I felt like I had totally let go. There was a long stretch of nothingness. And then my head slammed against a piece of wood.

I opened my eyes and saw that I'd moved—bounced? flown?—across the room and hit a pillar at the center. Did I defy the laws of physics? No. Did I swoop across the room in some sort of enlightened swoosh? No. It almost certainly looked like the uncomfortable hopping I'd seen adults do as a kid. But none of that mattered to me at that moment. Without even realizing it was happening, I began to sob. Big, uncontrollable sobs. I was crying for the brevity of what had happened—and the terribleness of being snapped out of it, back here to this shitty foam and my shitty thoughts and this stupid piece of wood. I feel like I'd had a brief momentary glimpse of the universe. I'd like to say I wept from the beauty of what I saw, but it was more the terrifying and wonderful freedom of the vast black space that made me cry.

I was also crying for the harshness of what I'd come back to, the harshness of my own mind. I understood in that moment what my mom had been chasing, the pureness of what Maharishi had given her and why she'd let the pursuit of that feeling become the focal point of our lives. "It just feels good," she'd always say with a smile, as if she knew something I didn't. And she had known something. She'd known that things were so much more beautiful and strange than logic allowed. I crawled back to my corner of the foam, curled into the fetal position, and wept for a good long while.

I took the Flying Course because I wanted to change and it worked. After that, I felt something inside me soften. I was less sure about what was right or wrong. How could you be so sure of anything when you'd glimpsed the fabric of the universe in the middle of a crappy basement filled with foam? I understood something for myself that was monumental and felt like a key to understanding my life, past and present. I understood—immediately, in that moment—that in order to have a sublime experience you had to be absurd. That there was nothing logical about faith and believing and that despite what atheists might say, that was exactly the point. You had to let go of the part of you that was critical and logical in order to escape your own humanness. And sometimes you needed a way to escape.

*   *   *

Despite my remaining questions about his integrity, Maharishi had given my mother and me something valuable: a tool with which to temper the world around us. My fear that I was genetically predisposed to cynicism wasn't real. And I knew then that I would use his meditation technique for the rest of my life. I will always need the space and remove that TM provides me. I wasn't going to let it go again.

But as far as the great guru goes—I had to let him go. Had he been a man who experienced different states of consciousness and who shared that experience and the tools he used with others? Yes. Had he loved money and women and power? It appears he had. Why had we wanted him to be more than human? Why had he wanted to be more than human?

The Movement I had grown up in—call it a cult, a religion, a community, it was all these—had rescued my family from a scary time. We were sheltered from the darkness of our past—my father's addiction and abandonment, my mother's abusive history. We were given a sense of magic and mystery and superpowers— we believed we could control our destinies and the fate of the world.

And yet—it was unsustainable. Sooner or later our humanness, which we push away, gets shoved back. Maharishi retreated into an insular world and his demands became unbearably restrictive. I can't help but think that he was battling himself during this time, battling his own desires and urges, whether they were for power, or influence, or money. Is it his fault that we were listening and following his every word and wish? Donning turbans and sipping acerbic teas while living in a trailer park? In the end it was our belief in him that mattered.

*   *   *

When I asked four-year-old Josie if she wanted to learn to meditate, she replied with an enthusiastic yes, as if I had asked her if she wanted candy or ice cream. But when the date and time were set, and we were on our way over to the puja setting, she had a change of heart. "I don't want to meditate," she told me. "I don't like sleeping."

I laughed. Josie's image of meditation was me hunched over, slacked jawed in my bed. No, I reassured her, her meditation wouldn't be anything like sleeping. During her Word of Wisdom time she could walk around and play, or color. She just couldn't talk. "That sounds hard," she said pessimistically. "Let's see how it goes," I said.

We were finishing up frozen yogurt in Larchmont Village in Los Angeles, Josie picking at her pile of chocolate chip sprinkles one by one. We rushed off to the car, cups in hand, and drove to a busy residential street in Hancock Park where we stopped in front of a small, Spanish-style house with a little sloping yard and rose-bushes and a little blue sign that said "David Lynch Foundation." We rang the bell, and in a joyous swoosh, Bobby, the head of the David Lynch Foundation, and former right-hand man to Maharishi, opened the door, squealing with glee.

"Hooray!" he said. "I've been waiting all day for this!"

His excitement was contagious and Josie and I both bounced into the dimly lit living room. On the walls were large framed photographs of David Lynch with other famous meditators, among them Jerry Seinfeld and Russell Brand. Josie was spinning around in her new rainbow-colored dress and falling into my lap, snuggling her teddy bear. We had brought a puja offering: flowers from a street-side vendor on the median of Highland for ten dollars and two greenish-yellow bananas from Starbucks.

Bobby asked us to follow him down the hall. We walked past a little alcove, where a picture of Maharishi hung, in golden '70s tones, holding a flower. The spare well-kept room was decorated in yellow and gold—yellow walls, two large golden upholstered armchairs that faced a little altar set up in the front of the room with a photograph of Guru Dev and a puja set—beautifully worn gold containers that held incense, a little pot of camphor, a little container of rice.

Bobby invited us to sit on the floor, as if we were just a group of friends hanging out. He asked Josie if she ever felt stressed, although what would toddler stress look like? No, Josie said definitively. What about sad or unhappy? asked Bobby. No, she said again, sensing some sort of trap. Bobby quickly changed tacks. Hey, Josie, do you want to be great? Yes, she said, without pause. Okay, this is a special word just for you, a mantra that's called your Word of Wisdom, and it'll help you be great, okay? Okay, she said.

We stood up and Bobby placed the bananas in a basket in front of Guru Dev's photograph and then asked Josie to choose a flower from our street-side arrangement—she chose a red rose, and a lily for me. Bobby took the rest, crushing one of the roses in his hand expertly, gathering the petals, then began to chant, slow and gentle and soft. I felt deeply moved to think that the tradition my mother had learned four decades earlier, and then taught me, was now being handed down to my sweet, beautiful daughter. A family legacy. My eyes filled with tears as Bobby lit the incense, put the petals in the water, and burned the camphor.

He then asked me to leave the room; Josie was unfazed by my departure. I stood in the hall, near the picture of Maharishi, feeling emotional and proud and confused.

A few minutes later Bobby came out beaming. "She went so

deep, bam." I rolled my eyes—he was of course being hyperbolic, but he assured me that she got it right away and that she was inside drawing by herself. He opened the door and there she was, sitting on the floor, happily drawing stick figures on a large sheet of paper. She looked up at me, her eyes bright, and I felt like my chest was going to crack open. This is who we are, I thought—meditators.

We walked out, Bobby beaming. I thanked him and gave him a check. I would've done it for free, he said. I didn't want that, I told him. Too complicated, I thought to myself.

As we opened the door, Bobby stopped me. Remember, whatever you do, don't force it.

In the car I asked Josie if she liked it, meditating, and she said yes. "Do you want to know my secret word?" she asked. "Wait," I said, almost reflexively, "didn't Bobby say you aren't allowed to tell anyone?" "He said I could tell you and Dad," she replied confidently. "Okay, what is it?" And in her most princessy magical theatrical voice, sotto voce, she replied, "Wisdom."

I told her this couldn't be her mantra, that her mantra was just a sound. But she declared confidently that she was right and changed the subject. (The next day Bobby assured me she knew what she was doing.) That evening I suggested to Josie that she go to her bedroom and meditate. I loved the idea of her being lost in her Word of Wisdom. "No," she said flatly. What could I say?

Epilogue

I'm sitting in my office on a midsummer's day, trying to figure out how to end this story, but really, there is no ending. It turns out there is no single answer to finding happiness, a terrible thing to admit because this is the elusive truth I spent my childhood looking for. When I was twelve years old I figured out that Utopia didn't exist, and that the World Peace we pursued was a fantasy. But the quest for personal fulfillment—call it Enlightenment, twenty-four-hour bliss, satisfaction, inner peace—that was much harder to relinquish. In Utopia Park and at the Maharishi School and even at the dining room table with Stacey and Mom, we thought positivity and inner peace was what accomplishment looked like. And we were forever failures.

So was the Movement a failure? Were we made the fools? I don't think so. My mom and her friends, our community—they had a profoundly sincere and motivated desire to build a utopia and change the world. There were countless hours spent in that effort, plans beyond the imagination. They pursued a dream, and even if it was just a dream, what mattered was the believing. The willingness to believe is everything.

Today the campus of Maharishi's university seems like a relic from another era. It is not a utopia, and one of the hardest things to see are the staff members who have worked there for decades, giving their time and their lives to a cause that is no longer there. Their guru is dead and the fortune he amassed from his followers is being fought over in Indian probate court. And yet they seem awfully happy, like old sweethearts still in love fifty years later.

I've gone to meditation retreats and listened to countless talks and sermons by other spiritual and religious leaders. I love the insight and the pursuit of a meaningful existence. And yet, when someone stands on an elevated platform and tells people what life means, I still resist. Never will I be able to trust that anyone knows the answer for anyone but themselves. Real trouble ensues when anyone tries to say otherwise.

So here I sit, as anxious as anyone I know. I meditated this morning, and for the first few minutes, I felt jittery and distracted, thinking about the things I needed to do today. And then, somewhere along the line, I checked out. My brain stopped. And twenty minutes later, I blinked open my eyes and felt pretty good. I heard my new baby daughter cooing in her crib, and I went to pick her up. Her whole body quivered with excitement and she flapped her arms when she saw me, shrieking with joy. In her dark bedroom, the sound machine playing soft waves, I pressed my face against hers and she gave me a huge octopus-like kiss. "This is divine," I thought. "This is happiness." And then the phone rang. And the dogs started barking. I laid Vivian down to change her diaper and knocked over a bottle of milk on the floor. "Goddamnit," I muttered. The dogs kept barking. Vivian started crying. Things had turned, and the moment was over, happiness a ghost to chase.

I still meditate using the twenty-minute technique that I learned when I was ten. I never practice the flying technique; it's just too much. Ben started meditating last year, loves it, and rarely does it. In thinking about what it all means, I don't have an answer. But I know that for me, meditation provides a space that is uniquely my own, a mode of being that is totally separate from the ups and downs of the everyday. When I can make myself settle into that quiet, transcendent space, I'm reminded on a deep level of who I am and that feels really good, like a big glass of water when I'm thirsty.

But I've come to believe that part of being who I am is being uncomfortable. (Along with a profound mistrust of anyone who stands on a stage and tells you the Truth About Life.) It's a funny contradiction that was bred into me—an ability to transcend and a countervailing reaction to push out and question. These days I try to enjoy that contradiction rather than fight to have one side be right or wrong.

I want my daughters to learn to meditate when they are old enough. I want them to have that special sense that they are beings separate from their thoughts and the anxiety that is the world around them. But what I will tell them will be very different from what was told to me. "This is very special," I'll say. "And it will make you feel pretty good. For a little while anyway."

Do I have dreams of a happy ending? Of course. I like to imagine a midsummer twilight in a field in Iowa. The air is cool and the stars are twinkling in a purple sky. My father is there and he is strong and healthy and present. His eyes are looking at me; they aren't lost in some torturous loop of the past. My brother is there and he's as sweet and brilliant as he was meant to be. He's forgiven himself for not being ideal and he doesn't buy into the phantom Hoffman curse of escapism, addiction, anger, and unhappiness.

My mom is there and happy that we are all happy. Her eyes are shining and she's letting loose with gales of laughter at some wonderful joke that my handsome husband has just told her. Ben is thrilled to be there, not distracted by some sense that he should be more productive or be making the world a better place at all times. There's a truck like the ones we used to park at the townie bonfires, blaring a Willie Nelson song, something about living forever, the chords delicious and twangy. And my daughters, well, they are just as they are—unaware and unafraid of themselves, laughing and wild and free and open to the magic of the earth and sky that surround us.

Fairfield spreads out beneath us—brick homes, flower-covered porches, Little League fields ablaze, golden domes gleaming in the last light of day. The tall poplar trees in Utopia Park shimmer in the warm wind. Heavenly. We are all lifted up, above it all, so that we can see ourselves and each other and the infinite space that surrounds us and feel the quivering divineness of being alive, of being human.

Acknowledgments

This book was a long time in the making and so there are many to thank and with much enthusiasm. That said, I first want to thank my wonderful editor, Gail Winston, who has supported me and my story with unflagging patience. Without my exacting and hilarious agent, Elyse Cheney, this book would never have seen the light of day, and she, along with Adam Eaglin, have been the cornerstones of this project. The talented Nell Casey threw herself and her big brain at this project, and helped me elevate the storytelling. I also received an extra set of eyes from William Patrick, which helped me figure out the shape of this thing.

I've been lucky enough to have great writing mentors in my life, starting with my brilliant and beloved Cindy Lou Johnson when I was seventeen, proceeding on to Chris Drew and Nicholas Lemann. They were all very kind to me when they had no reason to be and all are a reminder to me that young people are worth the investment.

I am lucky or conniving enough to have a stable of friends who are world-class storytellers. They have walked me through this book and include Reza Aslan, Kevin West, Lawrence Wright, Amanda

Fortini, Amy Wallace, Geoff Bartakovics, Joey Fauerso, Samuel Freedman, Deirdre DeBruyn, Margo Lion, and Mark Fass. Dana Goodyear in particular pushed me when I was running on empty. A special thank-you to Judy White for helping me go back in time and return better off to the present.

My fellow Maharishi School alum Donna Schill did great research on this project as did Alex Rose—thank you to both of you for your hard work. The friendship of my fellow travelers on this journey has been vital and it was an attempt at discreet mercy that many of them don't appear much at all in this book, but loom large in my life—so thank you to Wellsie, Joey, Gyan, Eleanor, Dougie, Johnny, Ananda, Jeni, Arek, Mandy, Ed, Ron B., Courtenay, Jeff and Ann, Rohini, Genevera, Chris Z., and Chris C. and many others. I know you all have different lenses with which you view our shared past but I hope you recognize the one you read here.

I want to thank Bobby Roth for his openhearted invitation to me to keep Transcendental Meditation in my life, despite my cynical and questioning heart. It is in many ways thanks to him that I still practice—and enjoy—meditation today.

I want to thank my brilliant and beloved brother, Stacey, for showing me how to be different from everybody else and not care about the consequences. I am thankful for my father for helping me look at the world differently and also suggesting I could write myself out of my situation.

I am fortunate indeed to have married my amazing husband, Ben, who endured the years I spent down the rabbit hole of my past and I am so grateful for his unrelenting belief that this was a project worth doing.

And finally, I am filled with gratitude and penitence to my mother, for working doggedly to raise my brother and me right, and for her faith in humanity and human consciousness, and, most important for the purposes of this book, for allowing me to tell my story, which in the end is really just a bumbling, inept love letter to her and to the religious experience, even though it may not always feel like it.

About the Author

Claire Hoffman writes for national magazines and holds a master's degree in religion from the University of Chicago and a master's degree in journalism from Columbia University. She was a staff reporter for the *Los Angeles Times* and has reported for the *New York Times*. She serves on the board of her family foundation, the Goldhirsh Foundation, as well as ProPublica and the Columbia School of Journalism. She lives in Los Angeles, California.